A Browser's Book of Texas Quotations

Compiled by
Steven A. Jent

Republic of Texas Press

Library of Congress Cataloging-in-Publication Data

Jent, Steven A.
  A browser's book of Texas quotations / Steven A. Jent.
     p. cm.
  Includes bibliographical references and index.
  ISBN 1-55622-844-9
  1. Quotations, American--Texas--Dictionaries.   I. Jent, Steven A.

  PN6081.B76   2001
  976.4--dc21   00-051751
                                                           CIP

Printed in the United States of America

ISBN 1-55622-844-9
10 9 8 7 6 5 4 3 2 1
0101

All inquiries for volume purchases of this book should be addressed to
Wordware Publishing, Inc., at 2320 Los Rios Boulevard, Plano, Texas
75074. Telephone inquiries may be made by calling:

(972) 423-0090

To My Parents

Permissions

Dietrich, Marlene. *Marlene*. New York: Grove Press, 1989.

Dobie, J. Frank. *The Longhorns*. New York: Little, Brown and Company, 1941.

"Boy In Search of Something," from *Bound for Glory* by Woody Guthrie, copyright 1943 by E. P. Dutton, renewed © 1971 by Marjorie M. Guthrie. Used by permission of Dutton, a division of Penguin Putnam Inc.

Holland, Ellen Bowie. *Gay as a Grig: Memories of a North Texas Childhood*. Austin: University of Texas Press, 1963.

Ivins, Molly. *Molly Ivins Can't Say That, Can She?* New York: Random House, 1991.

_____ *Nothin' But Good Times Ahead*. New York: Random House, 1993.

Reprinted with the permission of Simon & Schuster from *Rickenbacker* by Edward V. Rickenbacker. Copyright © 1967 by Edward V. Rickenbacker, renewed 1995 by Mrs. William F. Rickenbacker.

Scarborough, Dorothy. *The Wind*. Austin: University of Texas Press, 1979.

From *Travels With Charley* by John Steinbeck, copyright © 1961, 1962 by The Curtis Publishing Co., © 1962 by John Steinbeck, renewed © 1990 by Elaine Steinbeck, Thom Steinbeck, and John Steinbeck IV. Used by permission of Viking Penguin, a division of Penguin Putnam Inc.

Contents

Contents

Contents

Acknowledgements

For the illustrations I am again indebted to the Institute of Texan Cultures and the Texas State Library; Chris Floerke of the ITC and John Anderson of the TSL showed their customary courtesy and efficiency, making a long list of requests sound like child's play.

Thanks again to my friends in the DFW Writers' Workshop, and particularly to Ginnie Siena Bivona—workshop colleague and revered editrix for Republic of Texas Press, and easy to work with in either role.

Introduction

For hundreds of years, Texans have had interesting things to say about themselves, their home, and the rest of the world. For that matter, people beyond its borders have had interesting things to say about Texas and Texans for almost as long. This book brings together some seven hundred noteworthy quotations from or about Texas, from the sixteenth century through the twentieth. Collectively they form a portrait of this unique place in the words of the people who have lived and created the Texas experience.

This is not a collection of quips, one-liners, and epigrams, nor does the cast of characters consist mostly of Great Texans. Speeches and drawing room conversation are represented here, but they contribute a tiny minority of the entries. Letters, journals, essays, newspapers, advertisements, songs, poems, even official documents like laws and military orders: All these have yielded their share of citations that are by turns entertaining, revealing, surprising, or damning.

In a book of quotations from Texas, we can expect to hear from all the standard characters of Texas legend, and we can count on some of the traditional big talk—much of it true, much of it not—that fuels the Texas mystique. But Texas culture is far more diverse than that, as the people and topics compiled here will demonstrate. A few samples picked at random turn up entries on education, show business, the weather, medicine, conservation, bootlegging, and high fashion, from people whose occupations range from poet to prostitute to president.

By no means did all of the people I quote here intend at the time that their words should be preserved, or imagine that they were worth preserving, much less anthologizing. This is not a volume of *Words for All Time*. I have tried to collect fragments that would illuminate the character of Texas as it has evolved over the years, and you will find that many of them come from people as plain as a struggling homesteader or from sources as unpretentious as a one-page prairie newspaper. For each entry that aims to mark a significant event, capture a profound idea, or showcase the author's wit, there is another that does no more than log the passage of everyday life, but with an insight and a directness that gives it a power of its own.

Still, Texas has certainly produced its share of dedicated writers. It has also brought out the muse in a number of articulate visitors. Several of these, whether locals or passers-through, appear repeatedly in this collection. As some of them may be unfamiliar, it is worthwhile to begin with a few brief portraits, to avoid having to repeat their stories every time we hear from them. To begin with the visitors from other lands:

Closely as Mary Austin Holley was linked to the early Republic of Texas—as a cousin of Stephen F. Austin and as a one-woman tourism bureau for immigrants from the United States—she cannot be called a resident. She never lived in Texas, and the total length of her visits here is measured in months. But in 1833, after her first stay, she published *Texas: Observations, Historical, Geographical, and Descriptive, in a Series of Letters Written during a Visit to Austin's Colony, with a View to a Permanent Settlement in That Country in the Autumn of 1831.* She added material, including a history of the Revolution, for a new edition with the more compact title of *Texas* in 1836. Her book is the earliest known history of Texas written in English.

William Bollaert, an Englishman, was an accomplished chemist, soldier, and engineer. In 1842 he visited Texas at the suggestion of a friend in the British diplomatic mission to the Republic. Although he was a prolific author, his eight-volume record of his two years in Texas was not published until 1956.

Landscape architect Frederick Law Olmsted was already an experienced world traveler when, in his early thirties, he toured the South from 1852 to 1857. On his return to the Northeast he published *A Journey Through Texas, or a Saddle Trip on the Southwestern Frontier*. Olmsted's deep hatred of slavery may have inclined him to portray other aspects of life in Texas with a satirical tone. Today his travel writings are of greatest interest to historians; his most enduringly famous creation is Central Park in New York City.

In 1872 *Scribner's Monthly* magazine dispatched Edward King, with illustrator James Wells Champney, to report on life in the South under Reconstruction. Through 1873 and most of 1874 they traversed every southern state and some 25,000 miles. The series, entitled "The Great South," was so successful that a publisher in Glasgow (Scotland!) issued it in book form as *The Southern States of North America* in 1875.

In 1961 John Bainbridge, a veteran of the *New Yorker*, combined and expanded a series of essays into *The Super-Americans: A Picture of Life in the United States, As Brought into Focus, Bigger Than Life, in the Land of the Millionaires—Texas*. In his analysis of the Texan mind as expressed in the loud, uncouth lifestyle of rich Texas wheeler-dealers, Bainbridge wrote with a sort of amused admiration, a mixture of acute scrutiny and affection. In his view, the Texas tycoons were merely living the way most other Americans would live if they were given the chance. Even so, all but a few Texans detested what to them read like just more snobbish criticism from another uninformed Yankee. In 1963 Bainbridge left the United States to live in England, but this is probably just a coincidence.

Now we can move on to some of the Texans who appear here multiple times. I don't need to introduce such modern figures as J. Frank Dobie or Larry McMurtry or Molly Ivins. But there are several others who may date too far back for most of today's readers to remember them.

Noah Smithwick came from Tennessee to Stephen F. Austin's colony in 1827, but his early years in Texas gave him a dubious character; he was expelled in 1830 as an accomplice in the escape of a murder suspect. He returned in time to serve in the 1836 Revolution and remained in Texas until his Union sympathies made it expedient to spend the Civil War years in California. With the peace he returned to Texas, where he lived until his death in 1899 at the age of ninety. His daughter Anna posthumously published his memoirs, entitled *The Evolution of a State, or Recollections of Old Texas Days*.

Land agent Jacob de Cordova emigrated to Texas from Jamaica via New Orleans in 1839. Within a few years the prosperous Odd Fellow was serving in the State Legislature. He acquired huge amounts of land, at one point as much as a million acres, and toured the Northeast lecturing on the advantages of settling in Texas—on land purchased through the agency of Jacob de Cordova and his brother Phineas. In 1849 he founded the town of Waco. His 1858 book *Texas: Her Resources and Her Public Men* was part Texas encyclopedia and part advertisement for his land sales.

John Salmon Ford took on the nickname "Rip" during the Mexican War, when he served in the army as an adjutant. One of his duties was writing death notices to families back in the United States; he often included a personal sentiment of "Rest in Peace," which he abbreviated "RIP" when time or space was short. In his long and varied career, Rip Ford served as a Texas Ranger, a Confederate officer (he commanded the Southern forces at Palmito Ranch, the last battle of the Civil War), a newspaper editor, and a Texas congressman. His reminiscences and historical writings were collated and published long after his death as *Rip Ford's Texas*.

In 1885 Charles Siringo published *A Texas Cowboy; or, Fifteen Years on the Hurricane Deck of a Spanish Pony*, a memoir of his career as a hand on a number of Texas ranches. His experiences included cattle drives up the Chisholm Trail and an encounter with Billy the Kid (whose biography Siringo wrote in 1920). *A Texas Cowboy* is the first important autobiography of a cowboy and a classic in the literature of the Southwest.

William Sydney Porter is better known as O. Henry, one of America's premier writers of short stories. Most of the entries in this collection date from his earlier years as a journalist in Austin, where he edited the *Rolling Stone* for about a year in the mid-1890s. Some ten years before, at the age of twenty, Porter had moved from North Carolina to a ranch in La Salle County, in hopes that the Texas climate would improve his health. His experiences there and in his work as a draftsman at the General Land Office in Austin would later be reflected in his stories, several of which take place in Texas. In 1896 Porter was indicted for embezzlement at the First National Bank of Austin and spent five years in a federal prison. His career as O. Henry began while he was still behind bars.

Charles F. Rudolph was the epitome of the frontier newspaper editor. In 1886, at the age of twenty-seven, he led his family to a cowtown on the Panhandle named Tascosa and founded the *Tascosa Pioneer*. For the next five years he was Tascosa's most energetic booster, forever printing confident predictions that it would become the economic hub of northwest Texas. But the Fort Worth & Denver City Railway bypassed Tascosa, and eventually even Rudolph had to face the truth. He closed the *Pioneer* but continued to edit other papers in Texas for many years.

And then we come to William Cowper Brann. My own small and informal survey indicates that Brann is virtually unknown today, even in Texas. One could not ask for a more striking illustration of the ephemeral and capricious nature of fame. In his lifetime, which ended in 1898 at the age of forty-three, Brann's reputation extended across the country. His monthly paper, the *Iconoclast*, reached 100,000 subscribers nationwide, an enormous circulation a hundred years ago, and especially remarkable for a periodical from wild and woolly Waco, Texas, a town which then had scarcely progressed beyond its "Six-shooter Junction" days.

The *Iconoclast* lampooned a wide variety of people and institutions, taking on not only politics at the state and national levels, but literature and the arts, women's suffrage, prohibition, and the stark economic inequities of the industrial age. (His abuse of racial minorities, though symptomatic of his time, would offend most readers today.) Any form of stupidity, sanctimony, or greed was fair game. But Brann's favorite targets were religious dogma and religious hypocrisy, particularly as practiced by the Baptist Church, and most particularly as practiced at Baylor University, situated conveniently at hand in Waco.

By the fall of 1897, Baylor officials, faculty, students, and loyal Baptists had taken all they were going to. On October 2 a gang of students kidnapped Brann, hauled him to the Baylor campus, and warned him to leave Waco. On the sixth he was still in town, and three men, including a judge, beat him severely.

He wrote of his adventures in the November *Iconoclast*, and there is no better way to introduce his inimitable style than with an excerpt from "Revolvers, Ropes and Religion":

I have just been enjoying the first holiday I have had in fifteen years. Owing to circumstances entirely beyond my control, I devoted the major part of the past month to digesting a couple of installments of Saving Grace presented by my Baptist brethren, and carefully rubbed in with revolvers and ropes, loaded canes and miscellaneous cudgels—with almost any old thing calculated to make a sinner reflect upon the status of his soul. That explains the short-comings of the present issue of the Iconoclast. One cannot write philosophic essays while dallying with the Baptist faith. It were too much like mixing Websterian dignity with a cataleptoid convulsion, or sitting on a red ant hill and trying to look unconcerned. Here in Waco our religious zeal registers 600 in the shade, and when we hold a love-feast you can hear the unctuous echoes of our hosannahs from Tadmor in the Wilderness to the Pillars of Hercules. We believe with St. Paul that faith without works is dead; hence we gird up our loins with the sweet cestus of love, grab our guns and go whooping forth to "capture the world for Christ." When we find a contumacious sinner we waste no time in theological controversy or moral suasion, but promptly round him up with a rope and bump his head, and we bump it hard. Why consume our energies "agonizing with an emissary of Satan," explaining his error and striving by honeyed phrases to lead him into the light, when it is so much easier to seize him by the pompadour and pantelettes and drag him bodily from the abyss? Some may complain that our Christian charity carries a razor edge, that we skim the cream off our milk of human kindness then put the can under an alkali pump before serving it to our customers as a prime article; but bless God! they can scarce expect to

> *". . . be carried to the skies*
> *On flowery beds of ease,*
> *Whilst others fight to win the prize*
> *And sail through bloody seas."*

My Baptist brethren desired to send me as a missionary to foreign lands, and their invitation was so urgent, their expressions of regard so fervent that I am now wearing my head in a sling and trying to write with my left hand. Although they declared that I had an imperative "call" to go, and would tempt Providence by loitering longer than one short day, I concluded to remain in Waco and preach them a few more of my popular sermons from that favorite text, "If ye forgive not men their trespasses, neither will your Father forgive your trespasses." It is quite possible that a few heathen will go to hell whom I might enable to find the river route to heaven, but I believe in doing the duty that lies next my hand—in first saving the heathen right here at home. . . .

[T]he recent assaults upon me are not altogether my private concern. They were armed protests against a fundamental principle of this Republic—freedom of the press. They are being cited by ill advised or malicious persons as evidence of "Southern Savagery." They are calculated, if suffered to go unexplained, to cast reproach upon revealed religion. They were futile but brutal attempts in the last decade of the Nineteenth century to suppress truth by terror, to conceal the iniquities of a sectarian college by beating to death the only journalist who dared to raise his voice in protest. They were appeals to Judge Lynch to strangle exposure, hence it is imperative that the blame be placed where it properly belongs; not upon the South, which unqualifiedly condemns it; not upon the Baptist church, which indignantly repudiates it; but upon a little coterie of white-livered black-hearted hypocrites, any of whom could look thro' a keyhole with both eyes at once, a majority of whom are either avowed sympathizers with or active members of that unamerican organization known to infamy as the A.P.A. [American Protective Association, an anti-Catholic organization] *The same old God-forsaken gang of moral perverts and intellectual misfits who more than two years ago brought a Canadian courtesan and an unfrocked priest to Waco to lecture on A.P.A'ism, and who threatened at one of these buzzard-feasts to mob me for calling the latter a cowardly liar, were responsible for my being dragged with a rope by several hundreds hoodlums up and down a Baptist college campus in this city Oct. 2, and for the brutal assault upon me five days later by a pack of would-be assassins who had waited until my back was unsuspectingly turned before they had the nerve to get out their guns. I can overlook the assault made by the college students, although most of them were grown men, because they were encouraged thereto by their elders. I have positively refused to prosecute them; but the last assault was led by a shyster lawyer of middle-age, a so-called "judge," a member of the board of managers of*

Baylor. I am seeking no trouble with any of them—they are perfectly safe in so far as I am concerned; still if the latter gang are not satisfied with their cowardly crime, if they regret that they were beaten off ere they quite succeeded in sending me to Kingdom Come, they have only to notify me where and when they can be found alone, and I'll give the whole accursed mob a show for their money. I'm too slight for a slug- ger—cannot lick a herd of steers with one pair o' hands; but I can make a shot-gun sing Come to Christ. I am credibly informed that "at least half a dozen" of my meek and lowly Baptist brethren are but awaiting an opportunity to assassinate me, and that if successful they will plead in extenuation that I "have slandered Southern women." I walk the streets of Waco day by day, and I walk them alone. Let these cur-ristians shoot me in the back if they dare, then plead that damn- ing lie as excuse for their craven cowardice. If the decent people of this community fail to chase them to their holes and feed their viscera to the dogs, then I'd rather be dead and in Hades forever than alive in Waco a single day. . . .

I don't know whether Brann actually foresaw that he would be gunned down, but that is what happened. On the afternoon of April 1, 1898, he and Captain Tom Davis, another outspoken friend of Baylor, passed each other on Fourth Street. They may have exchanged words, or they may have just exchanged glares. But seconds later Davis pulled out a pistol and shot Brann in the back "where his suspenders crossed"—I have yet to read an account that fails to use this phrase. Brann, as he had promised, was also armed; he instantly turned, drew his revolver, and emptied every chamber, hitting Davis with all six shots, while Davis continued to fire, hitting Brann twice more. Both men lingered in agony before dying the next day.

The *Iconoclast* died with Brann; strangely, by the time the new century was in its second decade, William Cowper Brann, whom I regard as a satirist of the same rank as H. L. Mencken or Ambrose

William Cowper Brann sits at his desk with a satisfied expression,
as if he has just enjoyed skewering another Baptist.

Baylor University, The Texas Collection.

Bierce, was virtually forgotten. I recently visited Brann's grave in Waco and only realized later that purely by coincidence I had been there on the second day in April, the 102nd anniversary of his death.

For two reasons, he appears in this collection more often than any other person. First, he was astonishingly prolific—a million words in forty monthly issues—and only a correspondingly large sample would allow you to appreciate the wealth of scorching commentary he left behind. Second, I just plain admire the man, and this is my opportunity to make a few more people aware of him.

I have organized these quotations alphabetically according to their subject matter. You will quickly notice, however, that the subject headings are shamelessly whimsical, in keeping with the Texas tradition of eccentricity (or contrariness). Those who desire a more systematic approach will be pleased to find at the back of the book an index by author. But don't forget: this is *A Browser's Book*, not *A Reference Book*. Every reader will be able to think of a favorite Texas quotation that should be here, but isn't. In my defense I can only say that each selection that made it into the book struck me as in some way representative of Texas as I have known or imagined it, and that this is an intrinsically subjective affair. If overall you get a genuine sense of Texas—of *Texanness*—then I am satisfied, and I hope you are as well.

One last thought: a global *[sic]* applies here. Wherever you meet an unconventional spelling, like "quicksotic" or "strickly," you can assume this is not a typographical error, but an accurate transcription. These oddities occur just often enough in the original documents that inserting all the necessary warnings would clutter too many pages. At the same time it seems to me that in silently correcting them I would detract from the authentic flavor of the text. So I have chosen the third alternative: leave them as they are, and let them further your appreciation of the different world that our predecessors lived in.

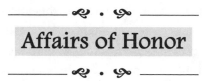

Affairs of Honor

Every person who shall kill another in a duel, shall be deemed guilty of murder, and on conviction thereof shall suffer death. Every person who shall be the bearer of any challenge for a duel, or shall in any way assist in any duel, shall, on conviction thereof, be fined and imprisoned at the discretion of the court before whom such conviction may be had.

> *Ineffectual law against dueling, 1836*

We had an affair of honor settled here yesterday, no blood shed however, all was amicably adjusted by merely shooting into WOOD. If all duels were settled by merely shooting at blocks, instead of BLOCKHEADS, the practice would be far more consonant with the dictates of wisdom and justice.

> *Dr. Francis Moore,* Houston Telegraph, *1837, after a duel between Thomas K. Ward and another man, in which both parties declared their honor satisfied when a bullet struck Ward's wooden leg*

Every steam boat that has come in from N. Orleans brings volunteers, and unfortunately not having Mexicans to fight with, have commenced fighting among themselves.

> *William Bollaert, diary, 1842*

From the "Caddo Gazette," of the 12th inst., we learn the frightful death of Colonel Robert Potter.... He was beset in his house by an enemy, named Rose. He sprang from his couch, seized his gun, and, in his night-clothes, rushed from the house. For about two hundred yards his speed seemed to defy his pursuers; but, getting entangled in a thicket, he was captured. Rose told him *that he intended to act a generous part*, and give him a chance for his life. He then told Potter he might run, and he should not be interrupted till he reached a certain distance. Potter started at the word of command, and before a gun was fired he had reached the lake. His first impulse was to jump in the water and dive for it, which he did. Rose was close behind him, and formed his men on the bank ready to shoot him as he rose. In a few seconds he came up to breathe; and scarce had his head reached the surface of the water when it was completely riddled with the shot of their guns, and he sunk, to rise no more!

> *In his* American Notes *of 1842, where he deplores the "fine mode of training" which encourages dueling, Charles Dickens cites a Texan newspaper's relation of the recent murder, during the war between the "Regulators" and the "Moderators," of Robert Potter—senator, former secretary of the Navy, and signer of the Texas Declaration of Independence.*

More often than otherwise, the parties meet upon the plaza by chance, and each, on catching sight of his enemy, draws a revolver and fires away. As the actors are under more or less excitement, their aim is not apt to be of the most careful or sure; consequently it is, not seldom, the passers-by who suffer. Sometimes it is a young man at a quiet dinner in a restaurant who receives a ball in the head, sometimes an old negro woman returning from market who gets winged. After disposing of all their lead, the parties close to try their steel, but as this species of metallic amusement is less popular, they generally contrive to be separated ("Hold me! Hold me!") by friends before the wounds are mortal. If neither is seriously injured, they are brought to drink together on the following day, and the town waits for the next excitement.

> *Frederick Law Olmsted,* A Journey Through Texas, *1857*

2

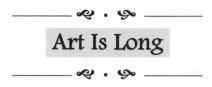

Art Is Long

Lone Wolf, chief of the Kiowas, was invited to an entertainment at Mangum on Sunday. For his special benefit one of the ladies gave a favorite selection on the piano. The noble red man listened patiently until she had finished when he said: "May-be-so me go, me sleepy." The effect of the remark can be better imagined than described.

> Quanah Tribune, *1894*

If I am correctly informed, God made the two men. I merely reproduced their likenesses. If you are dissatisfied about them, you should take the matter up with God.

> *Sculptress Elisabet Ney, replying to criticism of her monumental statues of Sam Houston and Stephen Austin, 1905*

They're simpler. You get them in a jam, and no one expects you to rack your brains inventing clever ways for them to extricate themselves. They are too stupid to do anything but cut, shoot, or slug themselves into the clear.

> *Robert E. Howard of Cross Plains, a suicide at the age of thirty despite his fabulous success as an author of fantasy stories, explains the primal appeal of Conan the Barbarian and his other creations*

Tend to the family, the diapers. Stay out of show business.

> *Advice from producer Billy Rose to Mary Martin, future star of* South Pacific, Peter Pan, *and* The Sound of Music, *1933*

I don't care whether I hit the right note or not. I'm not looking for perfection of delivery—thousands of singers have that. I'm looking for individuality.

> *Ernest Tubb, Country Music Hall of Famer*

I didn't want to be an actor. It was simply the best offer that came along.

> *Medal of Honor winner Audie Murphy, who starred in his own autobiography* To Hell and Back, *1955*

There are no political barriers to music. The same blood running through Americans also runs through the Soviet people and compels us to create and enjoy the same art.

I've become even more aware of this since I have been in Russia. What has thrilled me so much is the great spirit of musical unity achieved here at the Tchaikovsky Competition by the different peoples of the world whose governments are at political loggerheads.

> *Kilgore's own Van Cliburn, after he won the first annual Tchaikovsky International Piano Competition in Moscow, 1958*

I mulled the matter over for a few days and then sent Paramount a list of about a dozen titles; the best, as I recall, was *Coitus on Horseback*, a title I had long hoped to fit onto something.

> *Larry McMurtry, on the difficulties of picking a title for the film version of* Horseman, Pass By, *his first novel* (ultimately released as *Hud* in 1963), *from* In A Narrow Grave, *1968*

In the random way that democracy scatters art and monuments among its leaders, Lyndon Baines Johnson has a winner.

> *Ada Louise Huxtable, New York Times, on the Lyndon Johnson Presidential Library at the University of Texas in Austin, 1971*

...like saying only French people should do Racine or Molière.

> *Dancer and choreographer Alvin Ailey, on suggestions that his American Dance Theater should hire only black performers, 1973*

ORANGES FOR ENERGY
EAT ORANGES AND LIVE
LOVE ME, ORANGE, PLEASE LOVE ME

> *Messages embedded in the "Orange Show," an immense walk-through folk sculpture built from scraps and "found objects" by Houston postman Jefferson McKissack over the last twenty-five years of his life, and opened to the public seven months before his death in 1979*

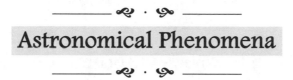

Astronomical Phenomena

To-night we made our beds under the canopy of the starry heavens, which shone so luminously that there was more pleasure in tracing the various constellations than in endeavoring to sleep. Every one must be struck with the extraordinary brightness of a prairie sky, due to the singular purity of the atmosphere.

> *Lieutenant James W. Abert, exploring the Panhandle along the Canadian River, 1845*

The stars, and especially the nebulae, do seem to shine more vividly, and to give more light and the firmament appears more effulgent than in any part of the northern or southern hemisphere in which I have been.

> *Frederick Law Olmsted,* A Journey Through Texas, *1857*

The very moon and stars are brighter, and flood the earth with molten silver that transforms even a red barn into a fairy castle, a piebald mule into a Pegasus, and falling between softly sighing trees upon the dark grass gleams there like fathomless pools in which you expect to see the heavens reflected.

> *William Cowper Brann,* The Iconoclast

The stars at night are big and bright.

> *"Deep in the Heart of Texas," June Hershey and Don Swander, 1941*

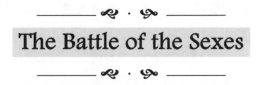

The Battle of the Sexes

TO WIDOWS AND OLD MAIDS

I trust that neither the young ladies nor their mothers will take any offense if I give a little advice to the widows and the old maids—although I do not suppose that in this assemblage of beauty there is to be found a decided old maid. Still, supposing that there may be some of these ladies who are thinking of emigrating to our State, I deem it a solemn duty to inform their friends that the gentlemen of Texas have always evinced a perfect horror at the bare idea of allowing the widow, and the old maid with her pet cat, to reside long within the limits of their State.

Our bachelors have entered into a solemn league to extirpate the whole race; and no sooner are they informed of the arrival in any neighborhood of either one or the other of these members of society, than they take the most energetic steps in their power to get rid of them, and are generally successful in their endeavors.

Having first got rid of the cats, they obtain the necessary warrant from the county clerk, and procuring the services of a minister of the gospel or of a justice of the peace, in an almost incredibly short space of time the ladies are compelled to renounce the cheerless state of single blessedness and are transferred, without much inconvenience, to that of matrimony.

Jacob de Cordova, "Lecture on Texas," 1858

Our young bachelor friend, Comer Nettles, came in from his old home in Wichita County last Monday. He brought in a clean bunch of fifty-one head of two year old heifers in fine condition. The young man is fixing for a sure living and a pleasant home. Maidens listen to the mockingbird.

Amarillo News, *1895*

The lectures at the court house by the phrenologist, Prof. Rupe, are drawing a good deal of attention, especially among the unmarried folks.

Quanah Tribune, *1895*

Marriage is, perhaps, the only game of chance ever invented at which it is possible for both players to lose.

William Cowper Brann, The Iconoclast

Jacob de Cordova, who represented the Republic of
Texas in the International Order of Odd Fellows as
the first Deputy Grand Sire for the new nation.

The UT Institute of Texan Cultures at San Antonio No. 68-2491
Courtesy of the Odd Fellows Museum, San Antonio

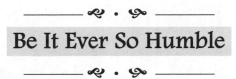

Be It Ever So Humble

Every farmer with an extensive estate lays out a town, which often consists solely of his own "castle"—far from being a castle *in the air* or Chateau d'Espagne, it is too often in the mud.

> *Mary Austin Holley,* Texas, *1836*

If you should have Carpenters imployed, I wish you to have a *Necessary House* built in the Back Yard, in the corner of the Fence by the Lane. It can be set over a dich; these *City Dames* will think it Horrible to run into the Woods.

> *Emily Perry, sister of Stephen F. Austin, writes to husband James at their Peach Point plantation in anticipation of a visit from cousin Mary Austin Holley, 1837*

Eve was delighted to see a nice walk from the gate to the front door, covered with shells. It did not look clean & nice very long, for I never saw anything like the mud here. It is tenacious black clay, which cannot be got off of anything without washing—and is about a foot or so deep.

> *Millie Gray, just arrived from Virginia, describes conditions at her new house in Houston, 1839*

The post was dilapidated; but the surroundings were far more agreeable than at either Fort McIntosh or Fort Duncan. A beautiful little river, the Leona, ran just behind the quarters, which were built of logs, and about ready to tumble down. We moved into a vacant house of four rooms; the kitchen was behind it, and was in an advanced stage of decay. A high wind might easily have blown it over.

> *Lydia Spencer Lane on accommodations at Fort Inge (near modern Uvalde) in the 1850s, in* I Married a Soldier

Our house was on the same order that most of the hunters used. They were called teepees made of buffalo hides. That was before dugout day. They were made as follows: first, we built a frame of small china poles, split some for rafters, no nails were used, rawhide strings instead. We took dried buffalo hides, tied the legs together and put them around the wall, wool side out, then another tier of hides over these in the same manner to break the joints of those underneath. The door was made of a frame of split poles with a buffalo hide stretched over it, legs tied inside. The little rock chimney with fireplace, which was crude, of course, came next. The floor was carpeted with buffalo hides, squared up to fit, wool side up. All was complete and a more clean and comfortable little home you could not find in any of the eastern cities.

> *Fifteen-year-old Ella Bird sets up housekeeping on the Panhandle with her buffalo hunter husband, 1876*

I wonder if any of you have ever seen, heard, or read of a "dugout"? I never had until I first visited my husband's ranch. You may depend on it, I was shocked to find not only cowboys but large families living in them apparently comfortable and contented. Can you of this de luxe age imagine people living in dirt houses? That was what a "dugout" was—just a good-sized square hole dug back into the south side of a hill. On the north side of the room, a special place was dug out to be used as a fireplace. Just above this a round hole was dug through to the top of the hill for the smoke to escape, and the cowboys called it the dugout chimney. On the south side of the room was an opening without doors that gave light and ventilation. There were no windows in the dugout and only a dirt floor. In times of storm a wagon sheet or tarpaulin was fastened across the doorway. It was in such a dugout that the cowboys spent their time when they were not at work on the range.

> *Mary Bunton describes the accommodations on her husband's ranch near Sweetwater in* A Bride on the Old Chisholm Trail *in 1886*

It was just a big square building: no screens on the windows, no indoor plumbing, a cistern to catch rain water for our water supply. Sometimes during the summer the cistern would go dry. When you turned on your faucet at the bottom of the cistern you got a pan full of wiggle tails [mosquito larvae]. Can you imagine why people had all those fevers? There were ants, there were ditches in front of the house where mosquitoes bred and crawfish grew. The streets were dirt with a little gravel mixed in. The dust was terrible. Can you imagine us coming from a big modern city to something like this?

> *Rose Keeper recalls the shock of moving from Buffalo, New York, to Houston in 1902 as a seven-year-old girl*

The way they fixed those things, they would put a wooden floor and wood around, up to about three and a half or four feet all around. Then they put a tent or tarpaulin and fastened down just below the top of this wood. Then they'd screen it in. They had to on account of the flies. They had screens up to the top.

And that was the sweetest sleeping you ever had. At night you'd just roll that tarpaulin up, and that breeze would just come through there, and it was the finest sleeping you ever see. Just a little bit shaky when it was stormy.

> *Tony Wilburn on the pleasures of life in a "rag house" in Pyote during the oil boom of 1926*

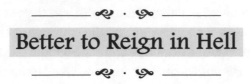

Better to Reign in Hell

I confess to a sneaking respect for Satan, for he is pre-eminently a success in his chosen profession. He's playing a desperate game against omnipotent power and is more than holding his own. He sat into the game with a cash capital of one snake; now he's got half the globe grabbed and an option on the other half.

> *William Cowper Brann,* The Iconoclast

I suspect that the orthodox heaven and hell, of which we hear so much, are Humbugs. I should know something of those interesting ultimates—be qualified to speak *ex cathedra*—for a doctor of divinity recently denounced me as a child of the devil. In that case you behold in me a prince imperial, heir-apparent to the throne of Pluto, the potential master of more than a moiety of mankind. But don't tell anybody that I've got a title, that I belong to the oldest nobility, or all the Goulderbilts will be trying to buy me.

> *William Cowper Brann, "Humbugs and Humbuggery: the Great American Product"*

Beware of Chicken

Going out in the chicken yard that morning I saw a Cochin China pullet with a young rattlesnake in her beak pursued by the rest of the chickens and muscovy ducks. In order that other witnesses might see this unusual performance I called to a neighbor and his wife and his cook and to my wife and cook, so that we would have six witnesses. By the time they arrived the pullet had evidently swallowed the young rattlesnake, but a Plymouth Rock cockerel had another, and he was being pursued like the pullet. My witnesses having arrived, I ran the chicken down until he dropped the snake. It was a young Texas diamondback rattler (*Crotalus atrox*) about twelve inches long, and it was still alive. I cut it in three pieces with an ax and the chickens and muscovy ducks fought over it greedily until every piece was swallowed.

> *Colonel M. L. Crimmins of San Antonio describes the snake-hunting skills of his chickens, in a 1931 number of the* Bulletin of the Antivenom Institute of America

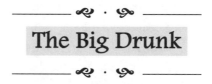

The Big Drunk

I gave Dr. Branch T. Archer of Virginia a letter of introduction to you; Dr. Archer has been in Texas upwards of twelve months, is intimately acquainted with matters and things there, and is in the confidence of all their leading men. He is of the opinion that there will be some fighting there next fall, and that a fine country will be gained without much bloodshed, he is very desirous that you should go there, and believes that you can be of more service than any other man; he left for Virginia today, and should you fall in with him, I expect that he will put you in the notion of going...

> *A letter from Texas patriot John A. Wharton to Sam Houston, then in Washington, D.C. as the emissary of the Cherokee nation, 1832*

AGREEMENT—The conditions are these: A. C. Allen alleges that Sam Houston will not abstain from the use of ardent spirits, wines and cordials; and should said Houston do so, then Allen is to pay said Houston...a suit of clothes...which shall cost and be worth $500.00; said Houston alleges that he is not to use ardent spirits, wines or cordials, and is only to use malt liquors, and should he violate this agreement, then...he is to pay the said Allen a suit of clothes worth $500.00. This agreement is to expire on the 31st day of December, 1838. The clothes are to be paid immediately thereafter.

> *Wager between Sam Houston and Augustus Chapman Allen, January 7, 1838 (Houston lost)*

I have never met an individual more totally disqualified for domestic happiness. He will not live with her six months.

> *Bernard Bee, in an 1840 letter (Houston's marriage to Margaret Lea lasted, apparently with happiness and mutual respect, until Sam died in 1863.)*

General and Mrs. Houston were taking breakfast. [Landowner and San Jacinto veteran Jesse] Walling was at the table. He inquired: "Mrs. Houston, have you ever been in Shelby County?"

The reply was in the negative.

"You ought to go there, madam. General Houston has forty children in Shelby County."

At this announcement the lady looked rather confused.

"That is, named after him," Walling added.

"Friend Walling," General Houston remarked, "you would oblige me very much by connecting your sentences more closely."

> *Sam Houston's bride of a few months, Margaret Lea, hears a startling statistic about her husband in 1840 Nacogdoches, in* Rip Ford's Texas

Margaret Lea Houston, in an engraving that suggests the stoic, patient faith with which she civilized her husband Sam.

Texas State Library and Archives Commission

Drunk in a ditch [Houston] is worth a thousand of [Mirabeau B.] Lamar or [David G.] Burnet.
> *Editorial during Houston's campaign for a second term as president, 1841*

I can regard Texas as very little more than Big Drunk's big Ranch.
> *Mirabeau B. Lamar, 1847*

The "Hero of San Jacinto" is not much troubled with mauvaise honte. He is a fine-looking man and would not be taken for more than fifty years of age although he must be near sixty. In his

15

rollicking speech on Friday night in the park, he told some capital stories and laid bait for complimentary notices with singular adroitness. "I have come to this city [Washington, D.C.]," said he, "the companion of men far more distinguished in the history of my country than myself."

Here, of course, there were loud cries of "No!" "No!" "No!"

"Well, gentlemen," said the Senator from Texas, "as you please. There was once a boy who came home drunk to his mother, and when she scolded him, he vowed that 'they had forced it down me.' 'Pshaw,' said his mother, 'I don't believe it.' 'Well, mother,' said he, 'they were going to force it down me, and so, seeing that, I took it freely.'

"Now, gentlemen," said Gen. Houston, "seeing that you will force this distinction down me, I'll take it freely."

The story was admirably eked out with staggering and hiccoughing, as "natural as life." Gen. Houston would make a first rate comedian, should all other trades fail.

> New Orleans Picayune, *1848*

Lord help the fish down below.
> *Sam Houston, upon being congratulated that baptism had just washed away his sins, 1854*

He was not a finished scholar—not a student of books; he was however, a thinker—a student of men and things.
> *Francis Richard Lubbock,* Six Decades in Texas, *1900*

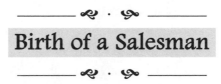

Birth of a Salesman

I was not completely without guile. West of Dallas, near Fort Worth, lies a small range known as "Chalk Hill." A major criterion of automotive excellence was the ability of a car to take Chalk Hill in high. Prospects naturally demanded that the demonstrations include this hill-climbing contest. We always made it, but one day, with a particularly heavy prospect aboard, I feared that we wouldn't.

In an effort to give the buggy every chance, I made a running start and we approached Chalk Hill at 30 miles an hour. The little buggy bounced and skidded on the gravel road like a skittish colt learning to gallop. We started up the grade, with my potential customer and me both leaning forward and pushing with body English.

Halfway up it became all too clear to me that we were not going to make it in high gear. Quickly I slammed on the brakes, and we came to a dead stop.

The customer turned to me, but before he could say a word I beamed at him with a proud smile. "How do you like those brakes?" I asked. "See how they hold us tight, right here on Chalk Hill?"

He smiled back. "By Gad, they do hold us, don't they?" he said. "Holy gee, that's great."

He bought the car that afternoon, for cash.

> *Future World War I fighter ace Eddie Rickenbacker, selling*
> *Firestone-Columbus automobiles in Dallas, 1909, in his*
> *1967 autobiography* Rickenbacker

Black Gold

Bituminous Lake.—Perhaps, a few of our citizens are aware that there is a small lake situated within one hundred miles of Houston, that is quite similar to the Pitch Lake of Trinidad. This singular lake or pool is situated in Jefferson County, near the road between Liberty and Beaumont, about twenty miles from the latter village. The lake is formed of Bitumen of Asphaltum, and about a quarter of a mile in circumference. In the winter months, its surface is hard, and capable of sustaining a person. It is generally covered from March to November with water, which is sour to the taste. Owing to this cause, it is called by the people in the vicinity, the "sour pond" or "sour lake." In the summer, there is a spring near the middle where an oil liquid (probably Petroleum) continually boils up from the bottom . . . This bitumen may at some future day become valuable as a substitute for coal in the formation of gas to light. It burns when lighted with a clear bright light, but gives out a very pungent odor.

> *In 1844 the editor of the* Clarksville Northern Standard *prophesies better than he knows as he speculates about the potential value of the oil in Sour Lake, which decades later fed one of the great Texas oil booms.*

Hurry, Anthony, something awful has happened. The well is spouting!

> *Caroline Lucas to her husband, Captain Anthony Lucas, after the Spindletop well erupted in a gusher, Beaumont, 1901*

How many men in the hurry, scurry, and irresponsible management in the field were taken out maimed, mashed, struck dead, will never be known. To get the oil out of the earth and get it converted to money was the sole thought of acreage owners; and those engaged in other forms of business were moved by like motives. They halted at no obstacles. Employers paid good wages for what they had done, and slam, bang, clang, they had to have results. Hence firemen with eyes so badly gassed they could hardly see the steam gauges worked around boilers; hence well crews worked with old rattletrap outfits that were liable any minute to fly to pieces and knock them to kingdom come; hence men worked in the top of derricks, hanging on with one hand, straining with the other to the limit of their muscles to adjust something that had gone wrong. After forty years of sobering absence, it still seems to me that there was more high-pressure work going on in Sour Lake than in any other place I have ever seen.

Charlie Jeffries remembers life, and death, in the Sour Lake fields in 1903

Oil, nothing but oil. It's water I want.

William Waggoner, head of the great 3-D Ranch (and eventually an oil millionaire), frustrated because his cattle can't drink the thick black stuff his drills keep striking, 1903

No matter what time of night you pass through the streets, you are sure to meet parties of negroes, who go where they please, unquestioned and irresponsible.

Houston Tri-Weekly Telegraph, *1856*

The people of Texas are informed that in accordance with a proclamation from the Executive of the United States "all slaves are free."

General Order Number 3 (origin of "Juneteenth"), issued by Major General Gordon Granger of the Union forces occupying Galveston, June 19, 1865

1. Do you belong to the White race?
2. Did you ever marry any woman who did not, or does not, belong to the White race?
3. Do you promise never to marry any woman but one who belongs to the White race?
4. Do you believe in the superiority of your race?
5. Will you promise never to vote for any one, for any office of honor, profit or trust, who does not belong to your race?
6. Will you take a solemn oath never to abstain from casting your vote at any election in which a candidate of the negro race shall be opposed to a white man attached to our principles, unless prevented by severe illness or any other physical disability?
7. Are you opposed to allowing the control of the political affairs of this country to go, in whole or in part, into the hands of the

negro or African race, and will you do everything in your power to prevent it?

8. Will you devote your intelligence, energy and influence to the furtherance and propagation of the principles of our Order?

9. Will you, under all circumstances, defend and protect persons of the White race in their lives, rights and property, against all encroachments or invasions from any inferior race, and especially the African race?

10. Are you willing to take an oath forever to cherish these grand principles, and to unite yourself with others who, like you, believing in their truth, have firmly bound themselves to stand by and defend them against all?

>   *Initiation ritual of the Knights of the Golden Circle, adopted 1868*

No man ever hung in Texas by lynch law was ever half such a criminal in the sight of God or man as the man who seeks to plunge his country into a war of races, the most savage of all wars, which would result in the extermination of the blacks and the ruin of the state. We say it solemnly, such men ought to die.

>   Houston Telegraph *editorial opposing the creation of black units in the militia, 1868*

I cannot give them too much credit for manly endurance without complaining.

>   *Lieutenant Colonel George Buell, in praise of the 9th (black) Cavalry Regiment's service in the Red River War, 1875*

Not very long ago I was making a journey between Dallas (Texas) and Houston. In some way it became known in advance that I was on the train. At nearly every station at which the train stopped, numbers of white people, including in most cases the officials of the town, came aboard and introduced themselves and thanked me heartily for the work that I was trying to do for the South.

> *Booker T. Washington,* Up from Slavery: An Autobiography, *1901*

Every time we have been in Texas we have had trouble.

> *Captain Lindsey Silvester, U.S. Army, a white officer of the black 24th Infantry, after the race riot in Houston, 1917*

As I understand the case, the Negro was guilty of doing something which he had no right to do. No, there will be no investigation by my department. He no doubt deserved it.

> *Dallas Sheriff (and Ku Klux Klan officer) Dan Harston, after members of the Klan kidnapped, whipped, and branded a black man, 1921*

Even a white man would have been lynched for this crime.

> *Governor Coke Stevenson, after a mob took black man Willie Vinson from a hospital bed and hanged him when a white woman identified him as her attacker, 1942*

Don't Trade Your Pride for a Segregated Ride.

> *NAACP Youth Council protesters at the 1955 State Fair, which still observed a separate Negro Achievement Day*

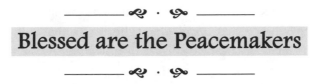

Blessed are the Peacemakers

Tom Smith has been Constable of Ozona, Texas for 23 years—and *never made an arrest or carried a gun!* Says Tom: "All I do is tell the boys to cool off—go home and think it over—after sleeping all night, take a good drink in the morning!—They feel so happy they let it go at that."

> *"Ripley's Believe It or Not," 1935 (Smith also never collected a dime in salary)*

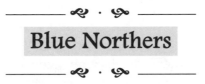

Blue Northers

(see **Storm of the Century** and **Texas Weather**)

Oh for a good cold norther! one of your real old fashioned ones, early though it be for them. We are tired of gazing upon burning, brassy skies; upon hot looking clouds, and the parched earth. We are weary of throwing open all the doors and windows, and placing ourself in the draught, in hopes to catch one breath of cool air to cool our fevered brow. We are weary of staying at home in the day time, lest we should be scorched with the intense heat; and of being obliged to remain within our mosquitoe-bar at night, lest we be devoured by the mosquitoes. We are weary of feeling the perspiration coursing down our cheeks as we sit at our desk puzzling our brains, or rummaging over the mails, in order to present something interesting to our readers. We are weary of the lassitude and languor; the constant relaxation of mind and body, which incapacitates us alike for mental and physical labor. We want something to brace us up. And what is better for that purpose than a cold norther?

> Houston Morning Star, *1839*

What not a day may bring forth may well be said of this day—it was cloudy but warm in the morning, like the Climate of Italy, at 9 A.M. the wind suddenly changed to the north, a severe Storm Thunder and lightning, with a tremendous rain, growing colder and colder every second—rain continued till noon when it commenced Snowing, and at 4 P.M. what was Italy this morning is now changed to Seberia, snowing and freezing.

> *From the diary of Adolphus Sterne, Nacogdoches, March 1843*

On the morning of my arrival [in Houston] I was inducted into the mysteries of a "Norther," which came raving and tearing over the town, threatening, to my fancy, to demolish even the housetops. Just previous to the outbreak, the air was clear and the sun was shining, although it was cold and the wind cut sharply. A cloud-wave, like a warning herald, rose up in the north, and then the Norther himself

> *"Upon the wings of mighty winds*
> *Came flying all abroad."*

It was glorious, exhilarating, and—icy.

> *Edward King,* The Great South, *1875*

A Texas norther, my Christian friend, may be, and usually is, very much of a nuisance. It is much like a spring day in Iowa—a cold, dank, windy, watery wetness. A norther is a Dakota blizzard that has gotten off the reservation and lost its bearings. It usually comes down on Sioux City first like a wolf on the fold, then makes a Fitzsimmons swipe at Omaha. Then it drops a tear on the pine tombstone of the erstwhile Jesse James and blows into the mouth of the Kaw just to see if it's loaded. It then starts across Kansas, but usually becomes frightened by the female reformers, and it comes a-chortling down into the Indian Territory and makes Lo the poor Indian yearn for a five-finger snifter of bootleg booze and a new government blanket. If it doesn't break its mainspring crossing Red River, it introduces itself to the people of Denison as a full-fledged Texas norther. The norther is bad enough in all conscience, but is to the blizzard what varioloid is to confluent smallpox, or lager beer to Prohibition booze. It is the thin edge of a northern winter which inserts itself into this earthly Eden semi-occasionally, much to our dissatisfaction. It usually catches a man seven miles from home without his overcoat. Sometimes it wanders as far south as Waco and evokes audible wishes that the Yankee would keep their d——d weather for their consumption.

   William Cowper Brann, The Iconoclast

At 9 o'clock Sunday morning the day was as pretty as one could care for. At 9:15 I had suspicions that I was in search of the North Pole.

   Cereal millionaire C. W. Post experiences his first blue norther in the Panhandle, 1906

Dear Sir,

While I still have got breath in my lungs I will tell you what a dandy car you make. I have drove Fords exclusively when I could get away with one. For sustained speed and freedom from trouble the Ford has got ever other car skinned and even if my business hasent been strickly legal it don't hurt enything to tell you what a fine car you got in the V-8.

Yours truly,
Clyde Champion Barrow

A letter to the Ford Motor Company, 1934

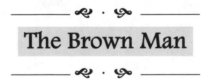

The Mexicans are very ignorant and degraded, and generally speaking, timid and irresolute; and a more brutal and, at the same time, more cowardly set of men does not exist than the Mexican soldiery. They are held in great contempt by the American settlers, who assert that five Indians will chase twenty Mexicans, but five Anglo-Americans will chase twenty Indians. The Mexicans are commonly very indolent, of loose morals, and, if not infidels of which there are many, involved in the grossest superstition ... There are many honorable and signal exceptions to this statement, it is true; but we believe the general character of the Mexicans in Texas and her vicinity has been pretty accurately drawn. Fortunately however, as we have seen, there are but few of the race within her confines.

> *Mary Austin Holley,* Texas, *1836*

We found much company on board on our return to the vessel, among whom was a contractor for beef for the army; he was from Connecticut, and has a family residing near the famous battle-ground of San Jacinto. He promised me some skulls of Mexicans...

> *John J. Audubon, diary entry from his visit to Galveston and Houston, 1837*

The Mexicans of Bexar are rather a diminuitive, and a very ignorant, lazy, dastardly, treacherous, and yet, apparently a harmless people. Their inferior character, however, is not in the least to be wondered at, and it would be a marvel were it otherwise, springing, as many of them have, from the prisons, abandoned soldiery, and worthless and vicious population of Mexico and Spain, and consisting, as no inconsiderable portion does, of the ragged relics of Santa Anna's miserable army, swept together from the streets, filthy lazarettos, and prisons of Mexico—conceived, nursed and educated in ignorance and villany, and purposely restrained and chained down to their natural degradation, by an imbecile, oppressive, priest-ridden, pusillanimous and semi-barbarous government. The great wonder is, that they are not a worse people than they look to be and really are.

> *Francis S. Latham,* Travels in the Republic of Texas, 1842

We have heard of men who speak lightly of robbing Mexicans but who would not entertain for a moment the idea of robbing an American. We do not believe in this doctrine. He who robs a Mexican will rob an American.

> Corpus Christi Star, *1848*

Common trials and dangers united the two races as one family, and the fact that one man was a Mexican and another an American was seldom mentioned, and I believe as seldom thought about. Each man was esteemed at his real worth, and I think our estimates of each other's character were generally more correct than in more artificial societies. Spanish was the language of the country, but many of our Mexican friends spoke English well, and often conversations, and even sentences, were amusingly and expressively made up of words or phrases of both languages.

> *William Wallace Mills, in* Forty Years at El Paso, *documents the use of Tex-Mex as early as the 1850s*

Frugal and temperate and fond of his ease, the Mexican sees no necessity for the wild turmoil and restlessness of his busy neighbors. He toils with moderation, he is satisfied with but little food, he cares not for luxuries, he takes his siesta when the sun is parching earth with hot rays. Not so the American. The latter eats and drinks almost ferociously. Like the wild beasts of the forest he must keep constantly moving. He is as avaricious and greedy as the sand of the desert. With inordinate acquisitiveness he struggles from earliest boyhood onward to add to his force. His only hope of temporal bliss is counting his hoards. He prays to God to bless his increase.

> San Antonio Ledger, *1853*

Q. Do you know of a desperado of the name of Rabb killing a Mexican on the Texas side some time in the summer of 1877? —A. I do; but I think it was in 1876. —Q. Where was it? —A. Out in Nueces County. This man Rabb was the son of a widow lady who is very wealthy. He was a desperado and a murderer, and was the terror of his neighbors, often of his friends. He became involved in a difficulty with some men said to be Mexicans, and he was killed. —Q. What took place after that? —A. His so-called friends, men living in that country, banded together and killed quite a number of inno-cent Mexicans. —Q. How many? —A. I should say not less than forty. —Q. Was there any report made of that? —A. I think not, although it is a well known fact in our country. —Q. Where were those Mexicans killed—in Mexico or in Texas? —A. In Texas; on the ranches, roads, and wherever they were found. —Q. What class of men were they? —A. Rancheros. —Q. Men of property? —A. Yes, sir. —Q. Were they killed indiscriminately, just as the bands happened to come upon them, or were they men who were selected to be killed? —A. It is reported that the bands killed them just as they came across them.

Testimony before the House Committee on Military Affairs, 1878

There is a large Mexican population here and I was astonished by the number of them bearing the name of Jesus. A young Mexican bootblack who wishes to cater for the American trade, at 10 cents a shine, asked a drummer for a Cincinnati house to paint him a sign, which he did, as follows: "If you want your boots shined, come to Jesus. Price 10 cents." The sign was removed in about two hours by a member of the Young Men's Christian Association and a less profane one put in its place.

San Antonio Express, *1891*

They accuse me and mexicanos in Cristal, in Cotulla and Carrizo Springs, of being unfair. One gringo lady put it very well. She was being interviewed around April 6, right after the school board elections and before the city council elections. The guy from *Newsweek* asked her to explain the strange phenomena that were occurring in these counties: a tremendous voter turnout and a tre-mendous amount of bloc voting. She said, "Well, this is just terrible! Horrible! A few days ago we elected a bunch of bum Mex-icans to the city council." And the reporter said, "Well, they are 85 percent of this county." And she replied, "That's what I mean! They think they ought to run this place!"

José Angel Gutiérrez, founder of La Raza Unida, 1970

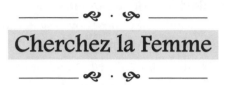

Cherchez la Femme

20 MARCH

...Tengo buena fortuna en al amor de la senorita—mosto una carta a ella sobre el conducto de la mujer de antes—[I have good fortune in my love affair with the lady. I showed her a letter about the conduct of my ex-wife.]

21 MARCH

...Spent day pleasantly—In la sociedad de mi inamorata—[In the company of my beloved]

28 MARCH

...Venereo mala. [Venereal disease bad.]

1 APRIL

...went to Cummins's—recepcion frio, pero conclusion muy caliente—[Reception cold, but conclusion very hot]

In his diary, the still-married William Barret Travis switches to Spanish to track the progress of his love affair with Rebecca Cummings in San Felipe, 1834

The Summer of Sixty I spent with a married sister at a little town in Coryell Co. Texas. While there I formed the acquaintance of an old bachelor who my brother-in-law thought a good match for me but I had no love for him and I soon discovered he was one of the most penurious men I had ever met and he always carried a Navy sixshooter. So I regaled myself every time he came to see me by getting his pistol under some false pretense and unloading it at a target I had set up. I was certain to get a good reprimand from my brother-in-law every time I did it for wasting the old bachelor's ammunition that he would think me so extravagant that he would never want such a wife. So this only made me more anxious to unload his pistol for him. So finally he ceased his visits entirely to my great relief.

> *Cornelia Evelyn Garner describes her ingenious way of discouraging an unwelcome suitor in 1860, when she was eighteen years old*

Compliments of W. N. Harrison to Miss May Moulton, and would be pleased to accompany her to a party this eve at the residence of Edward Schiff. July 22, '81. Greenville, Texas.

> *Future Greenville businessman and community leader Will Harrison courts his future wife, May, with old-fashioned formality*

I spent all my extra time when not on duty, visiting a couple of New York damsels, who lived with their parents five miles east of our camp. They were the only young ladies in the neighborhood, the country being very thinly settled then, therefore the boys thought I was very "cheeky" in getting on courting terms with them so quick. One of them finally "put a head on me"—or in grammatical words, gave me a black eye—which chopped my visits short off; she didn't understand the Texas way of proposing for one's hand in marriage, was what caused the fracas. She was cleaning roasting-ears for dinner when I asked her how she would like to jump into double harness and trot through life with me? The air was full of flying roasting ears for a few seconds—one of them striking me over the left eye—and shortly afterwards a

Charlie Siringo greets his readers on the title
page of the 1885 edition of *A Texas Cowboy.*

The UT Institute of Texan Cultures at San Antonio No. 73-902

young Cow Puncher rode into camp with one eye in a sling. You can imagine the boys giving it to me about monkeying with civilized girls, etc.

Charles A. Siringo, A Texas Cowboy, *1885*

Civil Disobedience

Sirs:

Since the information that you threatened to disfranchise your employees who failed to vote as you directed, we have this day made arrangements to purchase one of your wagons, "coal oil" the same and burn it in the presence of the voters of this precinct. The event will be duly advertised and published with a request that the press of the state copy the same.

We burn the "Studebaker" without knowing who will be president; we burn it in the same spirit that the tea was thrown overboard in Boston harbor in 1776 [actually 1773]; we burn it to commemorate the infamy you have heaped upon the workmen in your factory; we burn it that it may be emblazoned to Texas that you have placed a bulldozing bulletin on the walls of your factory, that we may condemn your lying cant and anathemetize your hypocrasy and that we may make your vile names odrous for all time to come, where liberty is known and freemen exist; we burn it to let our fellow countrymen of Texas know that we never desire to touch or handle any of your creations or make and that we consider the despicable coercion as treason; we burn it to consume the spokes, limbs, axles, etc., that have been made by the blood and sweat of victims whom you have reduced below the standard of manhood.

> Open letter signed by some 200 citizens of Dodd City, protest-
> ing to the Studebaker Company of South Bend, Indiana—
> then building wagons, later automobiles—which threatened
> to fire workers who voted Democratic in the 1884 election

A Corps of Rangers

An Ordinance and Decree to establish and organize a Corps of
Rangers...there is hereby created and established a Corps of
Rangers, which shall consist of three companies of fifty-six men
each, with one Captain, one Lieutenant, and one second Lieutenant for each company; and there shall be one Major to command
the said companies...
> *Birth of the Texas Rangers, 1835*

Me and Red Wing not afraid to go to hell together. Captain Jack
heap brave; not afraid to go to hell by himself.
> *Flacco, a Lipan-Apache scout, of Captain John Coffee Hays,*
> *1841*

Now, my boys, never after this say one and one make two, but five
and one make two; one Texan and five Mexicanos. This is
Rangers' arithmetic.
> *A ranger captain in Joseph Holt Ingraham's dime novel* The
> Texan Ranger; or the Maid of Matamoras, a Tale of the
> Mexican War, *1846*

The departure [from Monterey] of the Rangers would have caused
more regret than was generally felt, had it not been for the lawless

and vindictive spirit some of them had displayed in the week that elapsed between the capitulation of the city and their discharge...[W]e saw them turn their faces toward the blood-bought State they represented, with many good wishes and the hope that all honest Mexicans were at a safe distance from their path.

> *Luther Giddings, an officer of the Ohio volunteers,* Sketches of the Campaigns in Northern Mexico, *1853*

Imagine...men dressed in every variety of costume, except the ordinary uniform, armed with double-barreled shotguns, squirrel rifles, and Colt's six-shooters, mounted on small, wiry, half-wild horses, with Spanish saddles and Mexican spurs; unshaven, unwashed, undisciplined, but brave and generous men, riding pell-mell along roads, over the prairies, and through the woods, and you will be able to form a correct conception of a squad of Texan Rangers on the march.

> *Ranger Lieutenant Willis Lang, diary, 1860*

I have long since learned that each man on the frontier thinks just in front of his farm or ranch is the best place to post a company or detachment.

> *Ranger Major John B. Jones, 1874*

Any move in the direction of effeminacy or dandyism was put down by the boys. Once on a scout between the Nueces and Río Grande, and above the road from San Antonio to Laredo, an unlucky ranger, troubled with sunburnt and blistered nose and lips, hoisted an umbrella. Nothing was said or done the first day. The second day the captain took two men and went hunting. When they had gone quite a mile, a brisk fusillade was heard in camp. The two men were much excited: "Let us run back—the Indians have attacked the camp!"

The captain listened attentively for a while, and remarked: "No such thing—the boys are shooting Henderson Miller's umbrella."

It was shattered and torn into hundreds of pieces. The captain, for once, let the matter pass unnoticed. He did not see how he could remedy the affair, and thought that silence was wisdom.

In Rip Ford's Texas, *1885, we learn that, although the rangers did not have an official uniform, certain accessories were nonetheless considered inappropriate.*

Texline has been decided upon as the end of a passenger and freight division on this railroad, and will be built up by the combined effort of the railroad and the XIT interests, and there is a prevalent opinion that, as it is right at the line of Texas and New Mexico, close to No Man's Land and not far from the line of Texas and Colorado, it will be the biggest and the best and the fastest and the hardest and the busiest and the wildest and the roughest and the toughest town of this section. They've already had to station the Texas Rangers there and when that's said enough's said.

Tascosa Pioneer, *1888*

We drew a great many recruits from Texas; and from nowhere did we get a higher average, for many of them had served in that famous body of frontier fighters, the Texas Rangers ... They were splendid shots, horsemen, and trailers. They were accustomed to living in the open, to enduring great fatigue and hardship, and to encountering all kinds of danger.

Teddy Roosevelt on the Texas contingent of the Rough Riders, 1898

John Salmon "Rip" Ford, from a composite portrait of
delegates to the 1875 Constitutional Convention.

Texas State Library and Archives Commision

COME IMMEDIATELY. IMPORTANT. BRING YOUR
ARTILLERY.
> *Telegram from Colonel Ed House, of Woodrow Wilson's presidential campaign staff, to former ranger Bill McDonald, who replied "COMING," 1912*

Country Etiquette

My young friend, when you see anything of that kind going on in El Paso, don't interfere. It is not considered good manners here.
> *"Uncle" Ben Dowell—saloonkeeper, landowner, and postmaster—to newcomer W. W. Mills, after Mills tried to stop a knife fight in the town post office, 1858*

Don't fear to compromise your sex by attending the baseball game. It is affirmed on the best authority, that Mrs. Cleveland, now the first lady in the land, is enthusiastically devoted to the game. That should make it fashionable, and insure the game financial success in Texas.
> *In 1889, the second year of the Texas League, the* Austin Statesman *assures the ladies of the state that it is not a matter of scandal to be a baseball fan*

The St. Leonard Hotel is much frequented by Texas ranchmen, some of whom are not very refined in their habits. On the staircase, at the time of my visit, a notice was displayed requesting, "Gentlemen not to spit on the floors, walls or ceilings"; and the request was by no means unnecessary.

Mary Jaques on San Antonio manners, in Texas Ranch Life, *1893*

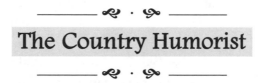

The Country Humorist

A young lady taking a walk one morning, met a gentleman of her acquaintance to whom she said, "You see, sir, I am out for a little *sun* and *air*." "You had better get a *husband* first" was the ready response.

Houston Morning Star, *1839*

"A lass! A lass!" as the old bachelor exclaimed, when he felt a desire to marry. He made the same exclamation after marriage, but spelt it differently.

Clarksville Northern Standard, *1843*

John Pimble's mule, Anatasia, died last week. Anatasia was standing in a field of popping corn which, due to the heat, began popping and covered the ground to a depth of 3 feet. The mule, thinking the pop corn was snow, froze to death.

Texas Panhandle, *Mobeetie, 1882*

I, A. B., in the presence of these my disgruntled brethern, do most sincerely promise and swear that Old Jim Hogg is personally and individually responsible for the drouths, cyclones, hailstorms, short crops and low prices of farm products in the state of Texas; and if [George W.] Clark is elected governor he will have the country in a worse fix than Hogg has, for I do solemnly swear that Clark is a bigger liar and a smarter man then Hogg.

I furthermore do solemnly swear and promise that I will not under any circumstances whatever vote for any man for office who can read or write or whose state or county taxes amount to more than $2 a year.

I furthermore do most solemnly swear by all that is good and bad, with all the devil and vim there is in me, that I do honestly and sincerely believe that the property accumulated by hard licks, industry and economy of our well-to-do citizens ought to be divided equally among the lazy, disgruntled members of this party and furthermore I swear that I will never be satisfied until this is done.

I furthermore tip-toe and rock back on my dew claws and most sincerely, solemnly, willingly and anxiously promise and swear that I never will plant more than half a crop of anything and will under no circumstances half work that, and I furthermore swear that I will do all I can to keep my neighbors from working theirs or paying debts, and to cap the climax I do with all the earnestness of my soul, from the bottom of my heart, sincerely promise and swear that I will take my wife's chickens, butter and eggs to town and trade for whiskey, get heap big drunk and talk politics.

> *John Bently Brown announces the oath of membership for his proposed alternative political party, 1892*

HUNTER When do the Texas game laws go into effect?

When you sit down at the table.

LAND AGENT Do you know where I can trade a section of fine Panhandle land for a pair of pants with a good title?

We do not. You can't raise anything on land in that section. A man can always raise a dollar on a good pair of pants.

ADVERTISER Name in order the three best newspapers in Texas.

Well, the Galveston *News* runs about second, and the San Antonio *Express* third. Let us hear from you again.

> *William Sydney Porter (O. Henry), "Queries and Answers,"* Rolling Stone, *1894*

Hill Decker Co. received an elegant new funeral car, which is a credit to any town. Everything is of deep black, even to the carvings. While it is the handsomest carriage in town, no one has yet expressed a desire for a ride.

> Dalhart Texan, *1905*

A man can sure stay all night quick at this ranch.

> *A passing cowboy who rode in at ten one night and woke with the breakfast bell at three the next morning, from the* SMS Ranch Booklet, *1919*

The only difference between a pigeon and the American farmer today is that a pigeon can still make a deposit on a John Deere.

> *Agricultural Commissioner Jim Hightower, 1986*

The Country Journalist

We have heard lately that there are a large number of persons in the Counties of Lamar and Fannin, who wish to take the *Standard* but who have no money to pay for it. It is a very easy matter for these people to arrange the price of a subscription. We will receive pork, cows and calves, honey or beeswax, articles which almost every man in these counties has or can command. We will also receive wheat or butter or cheese. Then, as to other objections as to the distance of transportation, neighborhoods could very easily send one person down with these articles from half a dozen persons without it being burdensome. We are disposed to be accommodating in this matter and we think that this arrangement will suit every man in these counties who wishes to subscribe.

> *Charles DeMorse, editor of the* Clarksville Northern Standard, *discusses alternative financing, 1843*

In the whole journey through Eastern Texas, we did not see one of the inhabitants look into a newspaper or a book, although we spent days in houses whose men were lounging about the fire without occupation. One evening I took up a paper which had been lying unopened upon the table of the inn where we were staying, and smiled to see how painfully news items dribbled into the Texas country papers, the loss of the tug-boat "Ajax," which occurred before we left New York, being here just given as the loss of the "splended steamer Ocax."

> *Frederick Law Olmsted,* A Journey Through Texas, *1857*

Why don't somebody kill a man, or get hashed up in a saw mill or something of that sort? It would be a terrible relief to newspapermen just now. If somebody could manage to get up a first-class scandal it would grease the wheels of local journalism wonderfully.

Fort Worth Standard, *1876*

The *Sun* can't please everybody, and sometimes fails to please itself. If you can't stand what it says cut the objection out and read the hole in the paper.

An exasperated editorial in the Williamson County Sun, *1881*

The *Tascosa Pioneer* tips its beaver to the good people of the great Texas Panhandle on this fair June morning, and settles down to business, we can only hope, as one of the permanent institutions of the section. The Pioneer is among you by invitation, we might almost say by creation, of the citizens of Tascosa and its neighbors; and to those citizens and those neighbors it must of course look mainly for its perpetuality. That it realizes this fact is sufficient guarantee on its part, we should think, for watchful and efficient service...

To conclude, we have no lack of faith in the future of our section, and while we are aware that a newspaper of this size will be looked upon by many as too large for such a town as Tascosa, we trust to the pride and liberality of our people and to its own energy and endeavors, to keep it up. Thus we take the future at what it may hold, and launch our little boat. Father Time will tell the rest.

C. F. Rudolph, editor, premiere issue of the Tascosa Pioneer, *1886*

I may be somewhat archaic in my ideas, but I hold to the theory that the mainstay of a paper should be its readers instead of its advertising acreage.

> *William Cowper Brann,* The Iconoclast

The *Iconoclast* is in its seventh volume and has never yet been caught in a falsehood or published an unclean advertisement. I am proud to say that no honest man or virtuous woman was ever its enemy, but that holy hypocrites and sanctified harlots regard it with the same aversion that a pickpocket does a policeman.

> *William Cowper Brann,* The Iconoclast

During the forty-five days ending July 26th, 56,971 lines or approximately $3,987.00 worth of undesirable advertising was refused all for the purpose of making the *Houston Post* "Your Kind of a Paper."

> *Publisher Roy Watson, a devotee of Christian Science, defends the* Houston Post*'s ban on advertisements for alcoholic beverages or patent medicine, 1918 (The lost revenue forced Watson to sell the paper six years later.)*

RESULTS

Thursday I lost a gold watch which I value very highly; as it is an heirloom. I immediately inserted an advertisement in your Lost and Found column and waited. Yesterday I went home and found the watch in the pocket of my other suit. God bless your paper.

> Dalhart Texan, *1920*

A newspaper may be forgiven for lack of wisdom but never for lack of courage.

> *Gene Howe, editor of the* Amarillo Globe-News *1926-1952*

SUBSCRIBE TO THE NEWS NOW

Hello folks, the *Kountze News* is just one day old. It's small, but give it time and it will grow, especially if you subscribe to it quickly ($2 a year)—Archer Fullingim, editor.

> *First issue of the* Kountze News, *1950 (published for the next twenty-five years)*

Joseph Pulitzer, they argued from city room soapboxes, never welcomed a smokestack industry to town with a page-one banner headline. Horace Greeley had not published an eight-column photo of one hundred and thirty-seven visiting oil executives. The *New York Times* did not devote its upper front page to an inspiring census report the day war began in Korea. Of course not, his supporters countered, and the *Chicago Tribune*'s Colonel McCormick had not mailed the World's Greatest Newspaper free to any soldier. Nor had Henry Chandler's *Los Angeles Times* printed verbatim trial testimony covering as many as seven full, open pages, and done it for ten straight days. William Randolph Hearst had learned to turn pages of his newspapers with bare toes and knew eighteen psalms by heart, but could he have driven a stagecoach down Wall Street? Yes, the Scripps and the Howards, the Copleys and the Knights, had comported themselves with dignity and regality while Amon stood on banquet tables and fired his six-shooters, but those men had only newspapers to sell, not towns, half of Texas, ideas, dreams, the future . . . glorious, magnificent, utopian visions. OK, but one couldn't imagine The *Times*'s autocratic Mr. Ochs pronouncing New York's highest elected official a "crazy sonovabitch" as Mr. Carter had of a Texas governor, and with an amazed audience looking on.

But I submit to you, was not that governor a crazy sonofabitch?

Of course, but...
> *At the death of Amon Carter in 1955, the reporters of his* Fort
> Worth Star-Telegram *debate his legacy, in* Amon: the Life
> of Amon Carter Sr. of Texas, *by Jerry Flemmons, 1978*

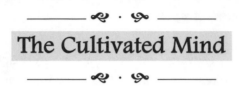

The Cultivated Mind

It is admitted by all that the cultivated mind is the guardian genius
of democracy and, while guided and controlled by virtue, is the
noblest attribute of man. It is the only dictator that freemen
acknowledge and the only security that freemen desire.

> *Mirabeau B. Lamar, "the father of Texas education,"*
> *address to Congress, 1838*

A wealthy planter says, "I'd rather be taxed with a poor boy's education, than for the poor man's ignorance, for one or the other I am
compelled to pay."

> Clarksville Northern Standard, *1843*

1st. You are not to use profane or obscene language about the college campus.

2nd. You are not to use ardent spirits, to treat others, or to visit
dram shops or drinking houses.

3rd. You are not to carry about your person or keep in your room
pistols, dirks, or any such weapons.

4th. You are not to play at cards or any game of hazard.

5th. You are not to be out of your room after 9:00. You are not to
engage in any nocturnal disorder or reveling.

Mirabeau Buonaparte Lamar: soldier, statesman, president
of the Republic, and Father of Texas Education.

Texas State Library and Archives Commission

6th. You are not to leave the institution without permission of the faculty.

> *From student regulations at Baylor University, Independence, 1851*

Universities are the ovens to heat up and hatch all manner of vice, immorality and crime.

> *State Senator James Armstrong, arguing (successfully at the time) against the creation of a state university, 1856*

I am well satisfied here. I am learning faster than I ever learnt in my life. My teachers returns their respects to you. We have excellant Teachers here they take all of the pains with the students that is necessary to advance them.

> *Baylor student Johnathan A. McGary Jr. shows off his progress in a letter to Johnathan Sr., 1859*

I hereby pledge myself, upon my honor as a gentleman strictly to conform to all the laws, rules and regulations of the Soule University, during my connection with it as a Student; cheerfully submit to the authority of the Faculty; to be punctual in attendance at Roll Calls and Recitations; to apply myself faithfully and regularly to my studies, and to give all proper aid in promoting the highest degree of discipline in the University; and I hereby certify that I have delivered to the President all of my concealed weapons.

> *Pledge required of all students entering Soule University, Chappell Hill, 1859*

Tell Ma I do not think she will ever send another child to France, if I am spared to tell my story. We are speaking nothing but French—everything I learn, music and all, is in French...Deliver me from boarding school of any kind, but particularly *French boarding schools*.

> *Sixteen-year-old Justina Latham of Houston writes home from Paris, 1864*

Come and live with and be one of us, and make your home and resting place, after a long and eventful public service, among a people who will never cease to love and honor you.

> *Governor Richard Coke offers the presidency of the Texas Agricultural and Mining College to Jefferson Davis, former president of the Confederate States of America, 1875*

The Texan of the old *regime* cannot understand how it is right that he should be taxed for the education of his neighbor's children; neither is he willing to contribute to the fund for educating his former bondsmen.

> *Edward King,* The Great South, *1875*

Ma I am sorry to say that this school is going down faster than I ever saw...I would not have said this but I heard two professors talking about it yesterday. They said in two more years that it would not be worth sending to. They are not managing it rite but I think it will last long enough for me to graduate...that is, I hope so.

> *Texas A&M student Lucius Holman, letter home, 1888*

In the court room this morning Judge Smith and County Attorney Osborne were freely quoting the Bible and Shakespeare, which made things not only interesting but also instructive to listeners.

> Quanah Tribune, *1897*

When you get an idea, don't run off into the woods with it lest somebody take it away from you. Put it on the anvil and bid the world hit it with the heaviest sledge. The more you hammer Truth the brighter it becomes.

> *William Cowper Brann,* The Iconoclast

You cannot estimate a man's intellect by the length of his purse, by the amount of money he has made and saved; but it is quite safe to judge a man's skill in his vocation by the salary he can command. I am informed that there has never been a time when the salary of the president of Baylor University exceeded $2,000 per annum—about half that of a good whisky salesman or advertising solicitor for a second-class newspaper. If such be the salary of the president, what must be those of the "professors"? I imagine their salaries run from $40 a month up to that of a second assistant book-keeper in a fashionable livery-stable. Judging by the salaries which they are compelled to accept, I doubt if there be a member of the Baylor faculty, including the president, who could obtain the position of principal of any public high school in the state.

> *William Cowper Brann,* The Iconoclast

Board of Regents, None.

We use no names of distinguished politicians or other men of high-sounding titles, for mere catch-traps.

Board of Trustees, None.

No such dignitaries to hold us in suspense for weeks or months when we wish to make the slightest change or needed improvement.

Board of Directors, None.

We are not check-reined by such a body of men who know far less about school work than about the business they follow, and who are ever ready to suggest ideas prevailing when they "went to school."

Board of Visitors, Everybody.

Who desires to attend college, or who has a son, daughter, or friend anxious to acquire a general and special education at a minimum outlay of time and money.

> *From the 1904 catalog of East Texas Normal College (now East Texas State University) at Commerce, founded in 1894 by William L. Mayo, who ran the school virtually single-handed for years*

I had rather resign the Governor's office of Texas than to have my children studying a textbook in the public schools of Texas with Lincoln's picture left out of it, and I am the son of a Confederate soldier.

> *Governor O. B. Colquitt, 1911*

The teachers couldn't stand it. They came and went faster than the worst people. It was just rough. They had some students that were rough. I remember one time in my class the teacher went to give a student a whipping. These barracks buildings, at the end of each one was a cloakroom. She took him back there and was going to give him a whipping, and she carried a paddle back there. He was a big boy. He pushed her around for a while. He didn't hurt her or anything, just frustrated her. He finally got tired of it and pushed the Sheetrock wall out of the side of the building and took off. That was the last time I remember seeing him in school.

> *Ruth Godwin on the flimsy schoolhouses and sturdy pupils in 1928 Wink, during the oil boom*

Ours was a reluctant civilization. Eastland County, Texas, had its share of certified illiterates in the 1930s and later, people who could no more read a Clabber Girl Baking Powder billboard than they could translate from the French. I recall witnessing old nesters who made their laborious "marks" should documents require signatures. A neighboring farmer in middle age boasted that his sons had taught him long division; on Saturday he presided from the wooden veranda of Morgan Brothers General Store in Scranton, demonstrating on a brown paper sack exactly how many times 13 went into 39, while whiskered old farmers gathered for their small commerce looked on as if he might be revealing the internal rules of heaven.

> *Larry L. King, "Redneck Blues,"* Warning: Writer at Work, *1985*

When the Board of Regents acted behind the closed door of Room 336 in the Rice Hotel at Houston, they tried a man without a public hearing. When they convicted that man of charges they will not list, the Board of Regents sentenced a great University to an infamy that makes meaningless its past and futile its future.

> *The UT student newspaper, the* Daily Texan, *on the arbitrary firing of President Homer Rainey, 1944*

The Board of Regents of the University of Texas are as much concerned with free intellectual enterprise as a Razorback sow would be with Keats' Ode on a Grecian Urn.

> *J. Frank Dobie, reacting to censorship of the UT student newspaper, the* Daily Texan, *1956*

I don't want to send them to jail. I want to send them to school.

> *Adlai Stevenson, on demonstrators in Dallas who assaulted him, 1963*

I didn't go to high school, and I didn't go to grade school either. Education, I think, is for refinement and is probably a liability.

H. L. Hunt, 1969

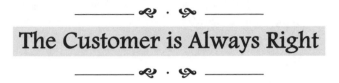

The Customer is Always Right

Rocking Chair Ranche Limd.
Aberdeen,
Collingsworth Co.,
Texas
May 31st, 1892

> Messrs Fore Bros.,
> Memphis, Texas

Gentlemen:

Please fill out the following order & get it out to our Headquarters Ranche on North Elm Creek as soon as possible. We believe our order will just about make a load for a two horse wagon: the freight rate of 60¢ is abominally high, for we can get freight hauled from Childress at any time for 50¢ & from there they have to cross Red River: do your utmost to get this rate of 60¢ lowered.

Take care that you put none of the articles ordered in paper sacks & mind that the flour is good for we shall sample it, & if bad return it. Mind that the fruit you send is good & not wormy, we shall examine it, & if bad return it. Also see that the molasses is in reality New Orleans molasses, we will not receive anything else.

1 sack green coffee
250 lbs canvassed strip bacon (not Armour's)
150 lbs granulate sugar

1000 lbs Wichita best high patent Flour
2 ten gallon kegs New Orleans Molasses
2 cases Lard, 5 lb tins if possible; if not, 10
150 lbs Navy Beans
100 lbs California Prunes
50 lbs Dried Peaches
6 boxes Axel Greese
25 lbs Rice
150 lbs Corn Meal
10 lb can best Mustard (Coleman's if possible)
10 gallons vinegar (not acid)
6 cases canned Corn
6 cases canned Tomatoes
3 cases canned Okra & Tomatoes mixed
1 case Coal oil

> Truly yours,
> Rocking Chair Ranche Limd
> By A J M

Archibald John "Old Marshie" Marjoribanks, not about to take any nonsense, orders provisions for the spread owned by his older brother, Edward Marjoribanks, Baron of Tweedmouth

The Dark Abode of Barbarism and Vice

The Sabine River is a greater Saviour than Jesus Christ. He only saves men when they die from going to hell; but this river saves living men from prison.

> *Anonymous outlaw, minutes after escaping American justice by crossing into Texas, 1835*

The most uncivilized place in Texas is I believe Houston the former Capital—I heard and read of more outrage and blackguardism in that town during my stay on the coast committed there, than throughout the whole of Texas. It is reckoned unsafe to attend the races there, or indeed to reside in the Town a week after them, so desperate is the Bowie-knifing and pistoling on these merry making occasions.

> *Francis C. Sheridan,* Galveston Island, *1840*

I regret that the beast forced me to do that which some ruffian ought to have done but I shall never regret that I killed him as I am sure he would have killed me.

> *James Pinckney Henderson, later the first governor of the state of Texas, after shooting "a desperado named N. B. Garner," 1841*

While their ostensible employment is this of catching wild horses, they often add the practice of highway robbery, and are, in fact, simply prairie pirates, seizing any property that comes in their way, murdering travellers, and making descents upon trains and border villages. Their operations of this sort are carried on under the guise of savages, and at the scene of a murder, some "Indian-sign," as an arrow or a moccasin, is left to mislead justice.

> *Frederick Law Olmsted on a class of brigands known as "mustangers," in* A Journey Through Texas, *1857*

On the 11 of March last, Wm. Sutton, my husband, and Gabriel Slaughter, whilst engaged in getting their tickets for Galveston, on board the steamer *Clinton* at Indianola, were murdered by James and Bill Taylor in my presence without any warning or notice, James Taylor shooting my husband in the back with two six-shooters . . . [T]he murderer of my husband is still at large and I offer to anyone who will arrest and deliver him inside the jail of

James Pinckney Henderson, first governor of the State of Texas.

The University of Texas, Center for American History

Calhoun County, Texas, one thousand dollars... Description of James Taylor, age 23 years: weight 165 or 170 pounds, very heavy set; height 5 feet and 10 inches; complexion dark; hair dark; round features; usually shaves clean about once a week; wears no whiskers, beard rather heavy, talks very little, has a low, dull tone, and very quiet in his manners. MRS. LAURA SUTTON

    Reward notice after one of many bloody episodes in the Sutton-Taylor feud, 1874

Six-shooter Junction! Thirty minutes for lunch and see a killin'!
> *Conductor's announcement when a train stopped in Waco, 1870s*

I was at my home and my own Dear Father told me never to put my foot in his house again and Brother Jim quit me and said I was too bad for him and my kinsfolk is all so G— D— cowwardly they don't want me to come about them so I stil alone tread the living land destitute of Friends, but G— D— the world and every son of a bitch that don't like me for I am a wolf and it is my night to howl. I expect to get killed some time but you may bet your sweet life that I will keep the flys off of the son of a bitch that does it while he is at it.
> *Bill Longley, murderer of perhaps thirty-two men, in a letter to Lee County Sheriff Jim Brown, 1877, written from "DevilsPass, Hells half acre" and dated "Septober the 41st, 7777"*

He said his name was McBride, but he was a liar as well as a thief.
> *Note pinned to the shirt of a man hanged from a pecan tree in Fort Griffin, 1878*

Tascosa has not had a man for breakfast [murdered] in all the two weeks' history of The Pioneer. This will be surprising news to a good many people on the outside, who thought we kept our streets always running crimson.
Tascosa Pioneer, *1886*

You can just say that I am a friend to any brave and gallant outlaws, but have no use for that stinking coward class of these who can be found in every locality, and who would betray a friend or comrade for the sake of their own gain. There are three or four jolly, good fellows on the dodge in my section, and when they come to my home they are welcome, for they are my friends and would lay down their lives in my defense at any time the occasion demanded and go the full length to serve me in any way.

> *Outlaw queen Belle Starr, interviewed in the* Dallas News, *1886*

Whenever you visit Austin you should by all means go to see the General Land Office...

Volumes could be filled with accounts of the knavery, the double-dealing, the cross purposes, the perjury, the lies, the bribery, the alteration and erasing, the suppressing and destroying of papers, the various schemes and plots that for the sake of the almighty dollar have left their stains upon the records of the General Land Office.

> *William Sydney Porter (O. Henry), "Bexar Scrip 2692,"* Rolling Stone, *1894*

He was polite and low-spoken, evidently a gentleman, but my sister and I felt uneasy and a little afraid. Maybe that was because we had never seen anyone with so many guns about him. Shotguns and rifles swung in their scabbards at the side of his saddle; broad belts crossed above his lean thighs, sagging from the weight of six-shooters and loaded cartridges. With somewhat of a sinking spell about my stomach, I also noticed the long knife he wore, which hung sheathed in its scabbard on his left side.

> *Teenaged Eunice Atkinson, homesteading in the Panhandle, is visited by an ominous stranger who she later learns was notorious outlaw Tom "Black Jack" Ketchum, 1898*

Some big-footed long-legged galoot with more stomach than conscience stole Prof. J. E. Farrow's watermelon Friday night. This was no ordinary watermelon. It was the pride of the Prof's. heart. Farrow does not regret the loss of the melon as much as he does the loss of the seed. If some of the seed will be returned to the professor no questions will be asked.

Dalhart Texan, *1907*

If not curbed, it will usurp the functions of the State and be destructive of government itself. It will indeed overthrow our Anglo-Saxon civilization in its relation to government.

U.S. Senator Charles Culberson on the spread of the Ku Klux Klan, 1923

It was not so much a matter of me being desperate for money as it was just being real damn mad at banks and bankers.

Bank robber and prison reform advocate Lawrence Pope, 1960

Dallas is a very dangerous place. *I* wouldn't go there. Don't *you* go.

Senator J. William Fulbright to President John F. Kennedy, October 1963

The murders are triggered by the most trivial irritations: last year a man was shot because he refused to lend another a nickel, and, more recently still, a gun-toter threw down on a waiter and shot him dead because there were too few beans in his chili.

Larry McMurtry on the crime rate in Houston, In A Narrow Grave, *1968*

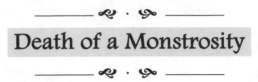

Death of a Monstrosity

The architectural monstrosity that has so long disfigured the crown of the heaven-kissing hill at the head of Congress Avenue, in Austin, is no more. The venerable edifice that bore such startling resemblance to a large sized corn crib, with a pumpkin for a dome, and whose halls have so often resounded with legislative eloquence, reminding the distant hearer of a dog barking up a hollow log, is gone...

It was a thrilling scene. The fire demon's cruel tongues licked the fair proportions of the historic pile, while huge volumes of black smoke poured from the doomed building, and settled over the fair city of Austin, like a sable funeral pall, enveloping in its somber folds the spires and domes that glitter on the seven hills of the Capital City of Texas, while the toot, toot, toot, of the fire engine, and the hoarse profanity of the enthusiastic volunteer firemen, seemed a solemn and appropriate dirge as the old sarcophagus crumbled into, etc., etc. But we are getting poetical, and encroaching on the province of the local reporter. What we have written in the above paragraph will, however, demonstrate that we can be sentimental and pathetic when we want to. Those who imagine that the Sifters have no pathos or poetry inside them are requested to read the foregoing, about the "doomed building" and the "funeral pall," over again...

When the alarm was given, it was supposed by a great many that the treasury, containing the million and a half cash balance, was in danger. The anxiety on the part of all classes to assist in removing the silver to a place of safety, was touching. Wealthy men, who had failed in business, got up from champagne and oysters, and, bareheaded, distanced impecunious candidates and seedy journalists, who were also rushing to the front to remove the cash balance to a place of safety...

> *The fire that destroyed the old Capitol Building in 1881, from the report that appeared a few days later in* Texas Siftings, *a satirical weekly printed in Austin (whose editors resented the fact that guards turned back "even newspaper men" who offered to help save the Treasury's silver)*

Demon Rum

Christmas day, a rainy, nasty, mean, day it is and the poor fellows who take a drop on Christmas are to be pitied, not a single thing in the shape of Liquor in Town.

> *From the diary of Adolphus Sterne, Nacogdoches, 1842*

Saloons will all be closed tomorrow. Very likely as usual, open at back door. As a general thing, there are more drunks on election day than any other.

> San Antonio Express, *1883*

Supper was called and the boys all rushed to the table—a few sheepskins spread on the dirt floor. When about through they missed one of their crowd—a fellow about my size. On searching far and near he was found lying helplessly drunk under his horse, Whisky-peet—who was tied to a rack in front of the store. A few glasses of salty water administered by Mr. Moore brought me to my right mind. Moore then, after advising me to remain until morning, not being able to endure an all night ride as he thought, called, "Come on, fellers!" And mounting their tired horses they dashed off at almost full speed.

There I stood leaning against the rack not feeling able to move. Whisky-peet was rearing and prancing in his great anxiety to follow the crowd. I finally climbed into the saddle, the pony still tied to the rack. I had sense enough left to know that I couldn't get on him if loose, in the fix I was in. Then pulling out my Bowie knife I cut the rope and hugged the saddle-horn with both hands. I overtook and stayed with the crowd all night, but if ever a mortal suffered it was me. My stomach felt as though it was filled with scorpions, wild cats and lizards. I swore if God would forgive me for getting on that drunk I would never do so again. But the promise was broken, as I stated before, when I received the glorious news of Cleveland's election.

Charles A. Siringo, A Texas Cowboy, *1885*

It was at the moment impossible, and on writing him my regrets, I offered to present an ornamental drinking fountain as a sop; but Roy Bean's quick reply was that it would be quite useless, as the only thing the citizens of Langtry did not drink was water.

> *Lillie Langtry is unable to work her namesake town, home of the eccentric judge who idolizes her, into the itinerary of her 1888 American tour (When she did visit Langtry in 1904, Bean had been dead nearly a year.)*

Water is an indispensable, but too much of it once wrecked the world.

William Cowper Brann, The Iconoclast

"The Fair will die!" Well, then, die, say we!
'Tis sad 'twere so, but had better be.
'Twere better dead and right soon forgot
Than one mother's son a drunken sot.
In tears, we'll mark her honored grave:
"The Fair is dead, but she died to save!"

> *Henry Lamar,* Dallas Dispatch, *in support of the movement
> to ban alcohol from the State Fair, 1916*

Hell, Judge, I've got that much in my right-hand pocket.

Then look in your left-hand pocket and see if you can find two years in the federal penitentiary at Leavenworth.

> *Galveston bootlegger Johny Jack Nounes and Judge Joseph C.
> Hutcheson Jr., after the judge fined Nounes $5,000*

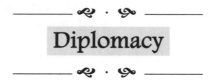

Diplomacy

Article I. Both parties agree and declare, that they will live forever in peace, and always meet as friends and brothers. The tomahawk shall be buried, and no more blood appear in the path between them now made white. The Great Spirit will look with delight upon their friendship, and will frown in anger upon their enmity.

> *From the Treaty of Tehuacana Creek, 1844, between the
> Republic of Texas and the Comanches led by Chief Buffalo
> Hump, who insisted on negotiating directly with President
> Sam Houston*

Lampasas, Texas
July 30th, 1877

Messrs Pink Higgins Robert Mitchell and William Wrenn.

Gentlemen:

From this standpoint, looking back on the past with its terrible experiences both for ourselves and to you, and to the suffering which has been entailed upon both of our families and our friends by the quarrel in which we have been involved with its repeated fatal consequences, and looking to a termination of the same, and a peaceful, honorable, and happy adjustment of our difficulties which shall leave both ourselves and you, all our self respect and sense of unimpaired honor, we have determined to take the initiatory in a move for reconciliation...

Lampasas, Texas
Aug 2nd, 1877

Messrs Mart. Tom & Sam Horrell

Gentlemen

Your favor dated the 30th ult. was handed to us by Major Jones. We have carefully noted its contents and approve most sincerely the spirit of the communication. It would be difficult for us to express in words the mental disturbance to ourselves which the sad quarrel with its fatal consequences, alluded to in your letter occasioned. And now with passions cooled we look back with you sorrowfully to the past, and promise with you to commence at once and instantly the task of repairing the injuries resulting from the difficulty as far as our power extends to do...

> *Proposal and acceptance of a truce (short-lived) in the Horrell-Higgins feud, mediated by Ranger Major John B. Jones*

El Paso, Texas, April 16, 1882

We the undersigned parties, having this day mutually settled all difficulties and unfriendly feelings existing between us, hereby agree that we will meet and pass each other on peaceable terms and that bygones shall be bygones, and that we will never allude in the future to any past animosities that have existed between us.

Dallas Stoudenmire

J. Manning

G. F. Manning

Frank Manning

El Paso Marshal Dallas Stoudenmire and the Manning brothers sign a truce, which ended five months later when George Felix "Doc" Manning and Jim Manning shot Stoudenmire to pieces in a fair fight

Don't Fence Me In

The cow hasn't been born that can run through my fence.
John "Bet-a-Million" Gates, barbed wire salesman

Light as air, stronger than whiskey, and cheap as dirt
Barbed fence company sales slogan, 1870s

Get up your scissors, boys,
And mount your gamest steeds,
There's work for us tonight,
To the prairies we will speed.
What right has bloated capital

To fence our prairies fair—
We'll cut the insolent wires
And make music in the air.
"Song of the Wire Cutters," Waco Examiner, *1883*

I have only one more chance with any hopes of stopping fence-cutting in this section & that is with my *dynamite boom* as I call it. I have had the law examined and it dont say any-thing about a man having the right to protect his property by the use of dyna-mite or by the use of a shot-gun either. So I have come to the conclusion if it was not against the law to guard a fence with a shot-gun to protect the property, it certainly would not be against the law to use dynamite for the same purpose. There-fore I have *invested some money* in *dynamite* & will in a few day's set my dyna-mite boom's upon the *few* fences that have been put up recently to protect them. Should the Gov. or the Genl. disapprove of this, all they have got to do is to notify me to that effect &c. They sent me here to stop fence-cutting any way I could, & to use my own Judgement &c. how to do it. And that is what I am doing & if they will let me alone the balance of this month I will have my boom's set & when the fence is cut, why they will hear of it in Austin.
Sergeant Ira Aten, Ranger Company D, Corsicana, 1888

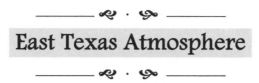

East Texas Atmosphere

The country where a midwife is a "granny woe-man"; one a 92-year-old mulatto woman with slender steely fingers who was said to have delivered a live baby from a dead mother. "White doctor say she daid, so I don't say she ain't." Signs saying "Wheels Spoked." Negro help leaping the fence to "git away fum de cunjerin' powder on de gate posts," placed there by some "cunjer" man or woman in the hire of an ill-wisher. East Texas, where they do things *right*, not cloddish. Negro children shouting "Santy Claw comin'? Santy Claw comin'?" when you want to take their pictures: "How he gon' know me on paper?" The stompin' ground of a blind, toothless guitar player: "Play me some blues." "I don' play no sinful songs, lady." His gigantic wife, Billie, emerging from out back hollerin' "An' me lookin' like Who'd-a-Thunk-It!" Razorback hogs and hickory nuts. Lightbread and sweet milk. English walnuts and Irish potatoes, and firecrackers at Christmas. The smell of fresh-made lye hominy, and the lacquered cypress beams of the smokehouse. A hint of frost in the air, and the sweet mouth of a coon dog when he trees.

Mary Lasswell, I'll Take Texas, *1958, on life in the Big Thicket*

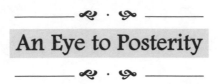

An Eye to Posterity

Be it known that I, Don Juan de Oñate, governor, captain general, and adelantado of New Mexico, and of its kingdoms and provinces, as well as those in its vicinity and contiguous thereto, as the settler and conqueror thereof, by virtue of the authority of the king, hereby declare that:

Whereas I desire to take possession of this land this 30th day of April, the feast of the Ascension of our Lord, in the year fifteen hundred and ninety-eight, through the person of Don Juan Pérez de Donís, clerk to his majesty, secretary of this expedition, and to the government of said kingdoms and provinces.

Therefore in the name of the most Christian king, Don Philip, the second of that name, and for his successors (may they be many), I take possession, once, twice, and thrice, and all the times I can and must, of the actual jurisdiction, civil as well as criminal, of the lands of the said Rio del Norte, without exception whatever, with all its meadows and pasture grounds and passes.

> *Explorer Don Juan de Oñate reaches the Rio Grande and crosses into Texas at the site of present-day El Paso*

There never was an enterprise of such great importance proposed at so little risk and expense.

> *René-Robert Cavalier, Sieur de La Salle, on his dream of leading an expedition to found a French colony in Texas (in which he was murdered and nearly everyone perished), 1684*

Madam, your land will be famed in history as the classic spot upon which the glorious victory of San Jacinto was gained!

To the devil with your glorious history! Take your stinking Mexicans.

> *Sam Houston and Peggy McCormick argue over the disposal of 600 Mexican corpses on McCormick's farm, the battlefield of San Jacinto, 1836*

LUCKY TASCOSA

Doubts and uncertainties are dissolved like morning mists! And the little city has only to go on to greatness! The Fort Worth & Denison is located to and through the town, and bright beams the future.

> Tascosa Pioneer, *1887 (By the turn of the century Tascosa was almost a ghost town.)*

I am the last leaf on the tree.

> *Mary McCrory Jones, widow of Anson Jones, last president of the Republic, 1901*

Keep your airport—it will place you among the commercial leaders of the world.

> *Charles Lindbergh, Dallas, 1927*

Houston, Tranquility Base here. The Eagle has landed.

> *First words transmitted to Earth from the Moon, 1969*

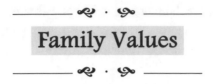

Family Values

I hereby order and command all the heads of families that they shall under no conditions consent, tolerate, or permit their sons and daughters to go together to bathe alone in the company of men, even though they be their own brothers, nor shall they go at improper or irregular hours, and those girls who are so found I hereby order whoever may see them bathing thus, to immediately inform me, so that I may proceed forthwith to place her in a safe place where she can be properly admonished; and I will permit only married men to go along with their wives to take such baths.

I hereby repeat my order that the women shall bathe at sunrise and the men after the tolling of the "angelus" in the evening, and whoever shall break any of the orders I have given shall be put in jail for ten days and shall pay a fine of six pesos.

Alcalde [mayor] Santiago de Jesús Sánchez of Laredo puts a stop to the wicked local custom of coed bathing in the Rio Grande, 1794

Were it possible for religious intolerance to destroy a nation, Columbia would soon pass from the map of the world, for in all God's universe there is not another so cursed with stupid bigotry and intolerant bile. If a man is a Catholic the Protestants want to disfranchise him; if a Jew he is compelled under pains and penalties to observe as the Sabbath a day which he does not consider sacred; if an Atheist he is ostracized politically and boycotted commercially; if a Deist he is between the devil and the deep sea, a target for the shafts of everybody, for the Christians fear him more than they do the Atheist, while the Atheists regard him as the

Hector of Superstition's stronghold. And this is "the land of religious liberty"!

William Cowper Brann, The Iconoclast

There are "good" people, yes, who might properly answer to the appellation "Redneck," people who operate mom-and-pop stores or their lathes, dutifully pay their taxes, lend a helping hand to neighbors, love their country and their God and their dogs. But even among a high percentage of these salts-of-the-earth lives a terrible reluctance toward even modest passes at social justice, a suspicious regard of the mind as an instrument of worth, a view of the world extending little farther than the ends of their noses, and only vague notions that they are small quills writing a large, if indifferent, history.

Larry L. King, "Redneck Blues," Warning: Writer at Work, 1985

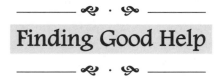

Finding Good Help

To the professional man we say that neither DOCTORS nor LAWYERS are wanted. We already have a sufficient stock in our market; and, were it not that some of them have been wise enough to turn their attention to farming and stockraising, a large number would starve, for there is not business enough in our country to support them...

To POLITICIANS we say, remain where you are; we have no room for you.

Jacob de Cordova, Texas: Her Resources and Her Public Men, *1858*

We, the undersigned cowboys of Canadian River, do by these presents agree to bind ourselves into the following obligations, viz—First, that we will not work for less than $50 per month, and we furthermore agree no one shall work for less than $50 per month, after 31st of March.

Second, good cooks shall also receive $50 per month.

Third, anyone running an outfit shall not work for less than $75 per month. Anyone violating the above obligations shall suffer the consequences. Those not having funds to pay board after March 31st will be provided for 30 days at Tascosa.

> *Declaration of the cowboys' strike in the Panhandle (which collapsed in a month), 1883*

He is the most helpless man I know, yet he is an honorable, good man but a fearfully and wonderfully made hanger-on for office.

> *U.S. Senator Samuel Bell Maxey wishes he could just find a suitable post for perennial place-seeker Andrew Jackson Dorn and be rid of him at last, 1883*

A pitiable sight was seen the morning after the flood. Six hundred men, out of employment, were seen standing on the banks of the river, gazing at the rushing stream, laden with débris of every description. A wealthy New York Banker, who was present, noticing the forlorn appearance of these men, at once began to collect a subscription for them, appealing in eloquent terms for help for these poor sufferers by the flood. He collected one dollar and five horn buttons. The dollar he had given himself. He learned on inquiry that these men had not been at any employment in six years, and all they had lost by the flood was a few fishing poles. The Banker put his dollar in his pocket and stepped up to the Pearl Saloon.

> *William Sydney Porter (O. Henry), letter, 1885*

We got in by train at about six o'clock in the evening. I got a taxi driver, and I said, "Do you know any place where we'd get meals and room for a few days till I get located?" "Yeah," he said, "I've got a friend that's running a rooming house."

He took me over there, and they put me in a room right off the dining room. While we were sitting there in the room, we could hear the men out in the dining room talking. I said to my wife, I said, "Them guys is drillers, tool dressers, out there." We got cleaned up, went out on the veranda. I said to the lady that waited on the table, I said, "Are those men all drillers?" And she said, "They're working out there in the oil field." South of Mineral Wells.

So we finished eating our dinner. I went out and set down beside a guy, and I said, "Do you guys—is there any drilling going on real handy?"

"Yeah," he said, "there is a boom out here south of town." He said, "Are you a driller?"

I said, "Yes, I am."

He said, "Are you looking for a job?"

I said, "That's what I come out here for."

He said, "The tool pusher is uptown hunting for a driller to go out tonight at midnight."

I said, "I've been riding the train and haven't slept any for five days. I wouldn't be fit to go out tonight and stay awake."

He says, "C'mon, we'll walk up the street, and see if we can find him."

And we started up the street, and we met him. And that guy hired me in one minute to go out at midnight.

> *W. H. "Steamboat" Fulton, looking for work and finding it a little quicker than he hoped, in Mineral Wells in 1919*

Bose Ikard served with me four years on the Goodnight-Loving Trail, never shirked a duty or disobeyed an order, rode with me in many stampedes, participated in three engagements with Comanches, splendid behavior.

Charles Goodnight's epitaph of foreman Bose Ikard, 1929

Hell, I can work. I like to work. Born working. Raised working. Married working. What kind of work do they want done in this oil boom town? If work is what they want done, plowing or digging or carrying something, I can do that. If they want a cellar dug or some dirt moved, I can do that. If they want some rock hauled and some cement shoveled, I can do that. If they want some boards sawed and some nails drove, hell's bells, I can do that. If they want a tank truck drove, I can do that, too, or if they want some steel towers bolted up, give me a day's practice, and I can do that. I could get pretty good at it. And I wouldn't quit. Even if I could, I wouldn't want to.

Hell with this whole dam layout! I'm a-gonna git up an' hump up, an' walk off of this cussed dam place! Farm, toodle-do. Here I come, oil town! Hundred mile down that big wide road.

Woody Guthrie, Bound for Glory, *1943*

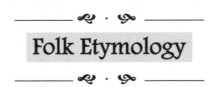

Folk Etymology

When every other land rejects us,
Here is a land which freely "takes us."

Houston Telegraph and Texas Register, *1839*

Texas (i.e. "the place of pro-tection"), so called in 1817, because general Lallemant gave there "protection" to a colony of French refugees.

> *E. Cobham Brewer,* The Reader's Handbook, *1898*

---

୧ · ୨

From Each According to His Abilities, to Each According to His Need

୧ · ୨

Instead of a life consumed by cruel anxieties, we shall have conquered at last the right of Freedom from Care, which results from the blessed sentiment of solidarity and which gives to each the consciousness that his individual life is integrant of the social life. It is the *right to social life*, the right to a harmony between the elements of life, and the being who lives. Each one here feels himself a member of a social body founded for his faith and by his faith, destined soon to realize this in its plenitude, and recognizes himself as an associate and an active agent in a work whose grandeur penetrates him deeper and deeper every day.

> *In his 1854 tract* "The Great West, A New Social and Industrial Life in its Fertile Regions," *French socialist Victor Prosper Considerant paints his utopian vision of a commune near Dallas called* La Réunion, *which, like so many other European ventures in Texas, was a costly failure*

Games Politicians Play

Since you have chosen to elect a man with a timber toe to succeed me, you may all go to hell and I will go to Texas.

> *Having lost his Congressional seat to peg-legged attorney Adam Huntsman, Davy Crockett takes his leave of Tennessee, 1835*

The most base, ignorant and vicious legislative assembly since the Rump Parliament.

> *President Sam Houston's assessment of the Texas Congress, 1844*

That lowdown scoundrel deserves to be kicked to death by a jackass, and I'm just the one to do it.

> *Congressional candidate, name lost, possibly mythical*

Take the unsavory stew of MacBeth's witches, season with ipecac, perfume with asafetida, and you get an *olla podrida* resembling Texas politics. We have Populists filled with pop and Prohibitionists full of prunes; we have two brands of Republicans, Mugwumps of every degree, and all kinds and conditions of Democrats. I am trying to perfect an apparatus that will enable me to photograph this Proteus of politics. It is the only animal on earth that goes forwards, backwards, and progresses to the right while it is moving to the left. It can turn inside out, swallow its own corporosity, sit down upon itself, and talk at the same time.

> *William Cowper Brann,* The Iconoclast

This is a fight between the common people and the privileged few, between democracy and autocracy. It is between the little country schoolhouse and the great university on the hill.

> *Governor Jim Ferguson, final argument in his impeachment, 1917*

Me for Ma. And I Ain't Got a Dern Thing Against Pa.

> *Campaign sticker for Miriam A. "Ma" Ferguson, 1924*

All for one and one for all.

> *Motto of the League of United Latin American Citizens, founded in Corpus Christi, 1929*

This race is not a matter of life or death for me. If I lost by one vote in an honest count the heavens wouldn't fall in. But about half a million Texans voted for me and they have been defrauded and robbed.

> *Former governor Coke Stevenson, contesting the results of the 1948 U.S. Senate primary election, which "Landslide Lyndon" Johnson won by 87 votes, thanks to the suspect Box 13 from Jim Wells County*

Tricky Dicky Nixon.

> *Archer Fullingim,* Kountze News, *1956*

We are not about to send American boys 9 or 10,000 miles away from home to do what Asian boys ought to be doing for themselves.

> *President Lyndon Baines Johnson, 1964*

We are trying to build a Great Society that will make your children and your grandchildren and the people three or four generations from today proud of what we are doing.

> *President Lyndon Baines Johnson, 1965*

He delivers The Speech almost casually, with infinite variations. He can recite it off the top of his head, forward, backward or from the middle.

> *John Ford, San Antonio* Express-News, *on Lloyd Bentsen's U.S. Senate campaign, 1970*

Ben is smarter than most of these other politicians. He wants cash.

> *John Orisio, former chair of the State Insurance Commission, to banker Frank W. Sharp, speaking of Lieutenant Governor Ben Barnes's participation in the Sharpstown corruption scandal, 1971*

Sometimes when you get in a fight with a skunk, you can't tell who started it.

> *Texas Senator Lloyd Doggett, 1984*

There's nothing in the middle of the road but a yellow stripe and dead armadillos.

> *Agricultural Commissioner Jim Hightower*

The Congress will push me to raise taxes, and I'll say no, and they'll push, and I'll say no, and they'll push again. And all I can say to them is read my lips: No New Taxes.

> *Presidential candidate George Bush, 1988*

I knew Jack Kennedy. Jack Kennedy was a friend of mine. Senator, you're no Jack Kennedy.

> *Senator Lloyd Bentsen to Senator Dan Quayle during the vice-presidential debates of 1988*

If anyone has any better ideas, I'm all ears.

> *Presidential candidate Ross Perot, 1992*

The Good Old Days

Elementary Studies, per term,	$13.00
Higher branches,	20.00
" ", including the languages,	25.00
Music on the Piano Forte, per quarter	15.00
Board, including washing and fuel, per month,	12.50

> *Student fees at Rutersville College, 1840*

You would be amused to know to what expedients we resorted to supply ourselves with the many necessaries which the blockade deprived us of. This ink is made of sumac berries boiled and strained—The bonnets and hats for men and women have all been homemade, some of corn shucks or husks or rye or wheat straw bleached split grain—then our gloves, if we had any, were spun, knit, colored, and all done by ourselves, in shoemaking I became quite adept particularly in the art of cobbling—We made our own soda, much of our toilet soap, and in all the different varieties of tallow candles I most particularly prided myself that I excelled my neighbor, the prickly pear hardening, alum clarifying, small twisted wicks, were all topics of conversation with visitors. But coloring was the great art of arts, the leaves, berries, bark and roots of every tree were tried, the long moss, short moss simmered and boiled. If sometimes when we expected a yellow or grey color, it came from the dye green or brown, we had only to try again with the hope of better luck.

> *Lucadia Pease, wife of former and future governor Marshall Pease, 1865*

[Telephone] Connections for the week ending July 23d 1881. Subscribers will please clip this out:

> 11. San Antonio Times.
> 17. J. T. Thornton, residence.
> 18. Ed Steves, residence.
> 25. J. H. Kampmann, residence.
> 42. Dr. John Herff, residence.
> 62. Dr. Amos Graves, residence.
> 63. Dr. Jos. Jones, residence.
> 64. H. D. Kampmann, residence.
> 68. Maverick real estate office.
> 72. Waterworks combination.
> 73. S. A. national bank.
> 74. Alamo mills.
> San Antonio Express, *1881*

I believe the best thing that can happen to a child is to be allowed to grow up in a small, pretty town. We had time to search for, and eat, sheep sorrel, peppergrass, and the nutlike seeds of bull nettle. We collected gal-catchers and the discarded chitinous cuticle of snakes and beetles. We stirred up doodlebugs from their dimple-like homes in sandy, protected spots. It was frightening to look at them under a microscope, and you had to be quick to see them before their weird forms backed off your hand. We were trick bicycle riders, and adept on the horizontal bar. The seats of our bloomers were usually very much in evidence. We played wolf-over-the-river, anti-over, and shinny, with a tin can and a crooked stick. I suppose these games have vanished with high-button shoes, pen-wipers, twelve-inch hatpins, and buttonhole scissors.

> *Ellen Bowie Holland, in* Gay as a Grig: Memories of a North Texas Girlhood, *1963, looks back on turn-of-the-century Weatherford*

I have witnessed in admiration the passage of shiny, new carriages of all types. One might note the English hack, the French barouche, the German landau, the low-aproned phaeton and carriage, or even the Irish dog-cart, the majority of them drawn by sleek-looking, high-prancing and thorough-bred horses.

> *Memories of Sunday afternoons in Houston's Sam Houston Park in the years before the First World War, from the* Houston Post, *1937*

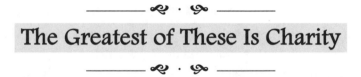

The Greatest of These Is Charity

He that gives liberally to the poor, to the church, to education, to the campaign fund, yet says to his brother, "Thou fool," because he's followed off after a different political folly, or differs from him on the doctrine of transubstantiation, is not staggering about under a load of charity calculated to give him flat feet. The supreme test of a charitable mind is toleration for the opinions of others—an admission that perchance we do not know it quite all. It is much easier to give a $5 bill to a beggar than to forgive a brother who rides his pitiless logic over our prejudices. The religious world has contributed countless millions to feed the hungry and clothe the naked, but has never forgiven Tom Paine for brushing the Bible contemptuously aside and looking "Through nature up to nature's God."

    William Cowper Brann, The Iconoclast

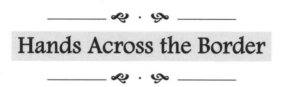

Hands Across the Border

Some of us had traveled six hundred miles to kill a Mexican and refused to accept a discharge until we got to Monterrey where a fight was awaiting our arrival.

    Private Buck Barry, 1st Texas Mounted Rifles, 1846

At last we have a real "sure enough" war on hand; something to warm the blood, and draw out the national enthusiasm. It seems that the "Magnanimous Mexican Nation" has at last come out of its chapparal of wordy diplomacy, treachery, meanness and bombast, and concluded for a little while, only a little while, to act like white people. There is at last—our pulses beat quickly with the thought—an opportunity to pay off a little of the debt of vengeance which has been accumulating since the massacre of the Alamo.

    Charles DeMorse, Clarksville Northern Standard*, 1846*

As Christianity is a living principle among a people, so do they stand forth in intelligence, freedom, worth and power. On the other hand, as infidelity pervades the spirit of a nation, in the same proportion has she sunk in the scale of political existence and moral excellence. For an example, observe the contrast between Mexico and New England: the one a perfect specimen of civilized degradation (if the expression may be permitted) and the other a rare model of the vital principles of Christianity, carried into every department of moral enterprise.

Melinda Rankin, Texas in 1850

It seems to me that the circumstances of the plunder of the stock ranches on the Rio Grande are almost identical with the piracies committed on our commerce at one time by the Algerines, who fled in safety to their own ports with their prizes. There the offences were committed on the open sea; here they are committed with the same ease on the open plain. In both cases the pirates found a ready sale for their captures in the ports where their expeditions were fitted out, namely, Algiers and Tripoli, &c, for the Moors; Matamoros, Reynosa, Camargo, Mier and Guerrero for the Mexicans. And in both cases the pirates were rewarded by promotions and honors.

Major General Edward O. C. Ord, commander of the Military Department of Texas, finds a historical parallel to the depredations of Mexican rustlers, 1875

Harmless Pleasures

The floor was cleared for dancing. It mattered not that the floor was made of puncheons. When young folks danced those days they danced; they didn't glide around; they "shuffled," "double shuffled," "wired" and "cut the pigeon's wing," making the splinters fly. There were some of the boys, however, who were not provided with shoes, and moccasins were not adapted to that kind of dancing floor, and moreover they couldn't make noise enough, but their more fortunate brethren were not at all selfish or disposed to put on airs, so, when they had danced a turn, they generously exchanged footwear with the moccasined contingent and gave them the ring, and we just literally kicked every splinter off that floor before morning.

> *Noah Smithwick describes the festivities at the wedding of two young settlers in the Austin Colony*

This atmospheric photograph of Noah Smithwick was taken not long before his death at the age of ninety-one.

The UT Institute of Texan Cultures at San Antonio No. 68-372

No paper will be issued from this office next week. The holidays are a season for comfort and recreation for printers as well as other devils.

> Clarksville Northern Standard, *December 26, 1844*

SHAKESPERIAN READINGS
Miss Ada Théodore,
Will give FOUR readings
from Shakspeare in this
place shortly.
Due notice will be given of 1st Reading.

> *In 1855 the* Liberty Gazette *announces a recital by the future Ada Menken: actress, poet, and courtesan, internationally famous for dancing in flesh-colored tights that made her appear nude*

Christmas week last year was one continual scene of mischief and drunken uproariousness all about town. Plows were perched to roost on the tops of houses. Signs changed their locations, and effigies of good and pious men were posted along the streets. This year all was peaceable, orderly, and quiet. The reason of this difference is obvious. This year the thoughts have been directed in a civil channel by parties and balls.

> *A newspaper clipping cited by Frederick Law Olmsted in* A Journey Through Texas, *1857*

Another form of amusement which might from time to time be conducted for a few minutes at table or about a camp-fire was a competitive reciting of the inscriptions upon the labels of the cans of condensed milk and other foodstuffs habitually used at the ranch. Partly for recreative nonsense and partly out of loneliness when solitary in camp, every cowboy sooner or later committed to memory the entire texts upon these labels and could repeat them verbatim. With a penalty of five cents for each mistake in punctuation, of ten cents for each error in a word, the competitive recitals offered a sporting possibility.

> *Philip Ashton Rollins, once a teenager on the trail from Texas to Montana*

The cattle season beginning, we think more freedom ought to be allowed, as everyone is aware of the amount of money spent in this city by the cattle men and cowboys, this making every business and trade prosper.

We notice especially this year that, contrary to their usual custom, almost all of them remain in their camps a few miles from the city, and give as the cause, the too stringent enforcement of the laws closing all the places of amusement that attract them, and thus their principal pleasures being closed and forbidden, they remain away from the city, paralyzing a large number of business houses and diverting from this city an immense amount of money which this city has always been the recipient of and benefited by.

We hope the honorable mayor and city council, who have always been foremost in the ranks when the city's prosperity has been concerned will see this in the same light and urge an enlightened view of the situation.

> *Open letter from "Many Citizens and Businessmen" deploring recent crackdowns on gambling and prostitution,* Fort Worth Democrat, *1879*

One night I shall never forget. The moon shone her best and brightest on a smooth stretch of canvas, spread so as to form a splendid dancing-floor, and on trees hung with fairy lanterns which extending as far as the eye could reach met as background the pretty little stream on whose banks lovers wandered. Of course, in that region of soft tropic warmth and fervor, romance blended with everything; and no eligible young lady was ever known to leave Fort Clark without a tiny circlet on her finger, which proved her right to return as an officer's bride.

> *One of surprisingly many pleasant memories preserved by Frances Boyd, the wife of a cavalry captain, in* Cavalry Life in Tent and Field

A Christmas tree is the subject of discussion among the little folks and older ones as well. El Paso ought to celebrate her first Christmas Eve in some praiseworthy way.

> *With the arrival of the Southern Pacific Railroad earlier in the year and the resulting influx of other elements of civilization, the* El Paso Herald *thinks it's finally time to observe Christmas like other people, 1881*

Did we have a dance? Just two days and nights. And did we eat! We had Delmonico beat two to one, for our chef was none other than Billy Dixon, noted scout, Indian fighter and hero of Adobe Walls fight.

Romance was in the air, so it was quite natural one of the handsome Turkey Track boys should toss his loop over one of our prettiest girls; wedding bells were ringing shortly after for two couples at least who were at the party.

When we got home we maybe looked and felt like the last petal of the last rose of summer in late twilight of a stormy day, but we wouldn't have missed it for anything.

> *Mollie Montgomery fondly remembers a shindig at the Turkey Track Ranch near Mobeetie, during the town's brief heyday in the mid-1880s*

Program for Cowboy's Ball

1. Grand circle round-up march	11. Cow and calf racquet
2. Horse hunters' quadrille	12. Night-horse lancers
3. Catch-horse waltz	13. First guard waltz
4. Saddle-up lancers	14. Second guard quadrille
5. Broncho racquet	15. Third guard Newport
6. Captain's quadrille	16. Fourth guard quadrille
7. Circular's gallop	17. Day herders' waltz
8. Round-up lancers	18. Maverick's polka
9. Cut-out schottische	19. Bull calves' medley
10. Branding quadrille	20. Stampede all

Taylor County News, *1886*

Everyone has a passion for chewing gum. The ostensible reason for the habit is its tendency to increase the natural flow of saliva, and thus to remedy indigestion. The gum is aromatic, and not unpleasant to chew, though the practiced chewer does not care for it in its original state; not, in fact, until he has rolled it in his mouth into a large insipid ball, resembling a lump of putty.

I have constantly found one of these balls of partially chewed gum between the joints of a rocker (chair), left there in this delectable form in readiness for future enjoyment.

Happening to pay a visit on one occasion, I received a great compliment; nothing less than the offer of a piece of gum direct from the manipulator's mouth, after she had taken all the trouble to make it "just nice" for me. I was assured that it had come all the way from Virginia, and was "real good." It was no easy task to escape the ordeal of placing it in my own mouth on the spot, and finding the most ingenious excuses unavailing to avert the reception of this fine (and perfected) Virginia gum, I thought that discretion was the better part of valor, and beat a hasty retreat.

Englishwoman Mary Jaques (who should have just been grateful that it wasn't tobacco), Texas Ranch Life, *1893*

Society anticipated, but its rosiest anticipation pales into the silver moonlight, rose radiance, charming details, graceful hospitality and women fair that made up the *tout ensemble* of the garden party given by Mrs. Hunter Craycroft on Tuesday evening. Had this delightful hostess gone into contract with the clerk of Old Boreas, she could not have been more favored. The evening was perfect. . . .

From a luxurious looking little alfresco stage, laid with velvet tapestries and piled with silken pillows, Mrs. Blanche Meeks Fallon told the story of *The Tar Baby and the Rabbit* and Miss Annie Lee Rodgers the story of *Lafitte's Treasure* so cleverly that smiles and tears played battledore and shuttlecock over the faces of the listeners . . . It was a night for coquetry and poetry and the beaux and benedicts alike felt the spell and wished—to the passing moment say,

Stay! thou art fair!

A brief but potent sample of Beau Monde's *description of an elite garden party in Dallas, 1896*

Yesterday [railroad magnate] E. H. R. Green startled Terrell by passing through the streets in his automobile, which is the first owned in Texas. The whole town turned out to witness the sight, dogs barked, horses were frightened and one child ran screaming into the house and told her mother to come quick and see the wagon running away without the horse.

Dallas Times-Herald, *1899*

Ye Olde Folk Singin Skewl
Will Practice at ye Domicile of ye townsman, Doctor
Clayton. Ax ye way from John Young
in ye Village of
OZONA
Ye People Wills Cum at Earlie Kandle Lite
By 7 hours past noon on ye sixth daye of ye week,
Friday, of ye third week in ye month in ye
ninth month of ye Yeare, September
21, during ye yeare of our
Lord, 20th centurye.
Ye Moneye will be for ye helpe of ye
METHODIST MEETIN HOUSE.
Ax ye waye from ye barn of Farmer James Brooks.
Cousyn Elam Dudley wille be special companie.
Ye Singer, Madam Cox, wille sound ye tunin forke.
Ye sires and ye dames wille raise yeir voices in
So-lows, Doo-etts, Kor-tetts and Ko-russes
Ye cost of comin in is fyxed at Two Shillings, or 1-4 Dollar.
Lads and Lasses, under 12, One Dime.
Ye merchant Henry Perner will acte as ye Door-Keeper.
Doctor Clayton will act as ye Seeter.
Ye Syngers wille robe Yemselves in ye Antikwe Toylet.
Cum ye One! Cum ye Alle!
Handbill for a choral benefit in Ozona, 1900

How-dee, Folks!
Big Tex, 1953 State Fair

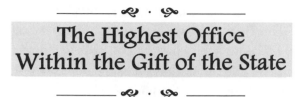

The Highest Office
Within the Gift of the State

Dear Governor:

You run things up in Austin and I'll run 'em down here.
> *Judge Roy Bean of Langtry, responding to criticism from*
> *Governor Jim Hogg, early 1890s*

A Texas governor has only two happy days: the day he is inaugurated and the day he retires.
> *Joseph D. Sayers, governor 1898-1902*

You have only three friends in the world—God Almighty, Sears-Roebuck, and Jim Ferguson.
> *Campaign slogan, 1916*

I will admit that the Supreme Being failed to favor me with physical attributes pleasing to Governor Ferguson, but at least He gave me the intelligence to know the difference between my own money and that which belongs to the State.
> *Governor William P. Hobby, running against impeached,*
> *deposed, and therefore ineligible former governor Jim*
> *Ferguson*

And now, Mrs. Ferguson, the fierce, critical, piercing white light which has beat for four years upon my path, will shine about you, as into your hands pass the duties and the responsibilities, the service and the sacrifice of the highest office within the gift of the State... On your working desk you will find the open Bible with verse marked: "Thy word is a lamp unto my feet, and a light unto my path." This Book of Books is my gift to you and to all your successors in office for their chart and compass while directing the ship of state. May the God who guides the migratory birds in their flight, and who holds within the hollow of His hand the destinies of men, guide and guard you, and hold and keep all Texas aright.

> *Outgoing Governor Pat Neff to Miriam A. "Ma" Ferguson, 1925, beginning the tradition in which every exiting governor leaves a marked Bible passage for the new occupants of the Governor's Mansion*

Roses are red and violets are blue.
If you love me like I love you,
No knife can cut our love in two.

> *The complete text of "Ma" Ferguson's inaugural address, after her election to a second term as governor, 1933*

The Vice-Presidency of the United States isn't worth a pitcher of warm spit.

> *John Nance Garner, vice president of the United States 1933-1941*

Just as I broke the news to him of his appointment, the sun suddenly shot through the dark rain clouds in such a fashion that it appeared dazzling. I said, "General, do you know what caused that sun to suddenly burst through those dark and heavy clouds? It appears to me as if our great and good loving God has just spread the clouds apart so the spirit of your illustrious father could smile down upon his son on this particular scene and see the big smile on your face."

> *Governor W. Lee O'Daniel to Sam Houston's last surviving son, Andrew Jackson Houston, age 86, after appointing him interim U.S. Senator, 1941*

You have to protect yourself shaking hands—it's really an art, a science, for a politician. You have to react very quickly. It's something nobody ever thinks about but it's awfully important when you do a lot of handshaking. For instance, some people make a quick grab and squeeze your fingers before you can grip their hands. That can really hurt. You have to be just a little quicker than they are and grab their hands first.

Some people, of course, try to overpower you; they really almost crush your hand. With a person like that, you have to grab his hand quickly and apply counterpressure, primarily with your thumb and little finger. I try to respond in kind and always have a fairly strong, firm handshake.

> *Governor John Connally, 1964*

High-Flying Texans

I will give a few ideas indicating generally the character of the air-ship and what it will be able to accomplish.

The AIR-SHIP consists of three main parts.

1. The lower suspended portion, formed like a ship with a very short prow to cut the air; it serves to hold the aeronaut, as also the power producing engine with all the steering apparatus. This portion is shut up all around to prevent the rapid motion from affecting the breathing of the man within...

2. The upper portion, or flying apparatus, which makes use of the resistance of the air, consists of a system of wings, partly moveable, partly immovable, presenting the appearance of horizontal sails, but having functions entirely different from the sails of vessels.

3. The portion producing the forward motion consists either of two screws, which can be revolved with equal or unequal motion, so as to serve the purpose of lateral steering, or of wings of a peculiar construction. The preference to be given to one or the other depends on the *force* of the motive power. Another apparatus *controls* the ascending motion.

In the Galveston Tri-Weekly News, *Jacob Brodbeck, a German immigrant of the San Antonio area, describes the airplane that he claimed to have built and flown in 1865*

Jacob Brodbeck, who supposedly flew a heavier-than-air craft more than thirty years before the Wright brothers.

The UT Institute of Texan Cultures at San Antonio
No. 68-703 Courtesy of Mr. E. E. Brodbeck

S. F. Cody measured the thrust of his aeroplane in 1908-1909 by tying it to a tree which stood here. Nearby he made his first tests with his powered aeroplane on 16th May, 1908, and his flight of 1,390 feet on 16th October, 1908—the first sustained flight in Britain.

> *At Farnborough, England, a monument records the achievements of Samuel Franklin Cody of Birdville, Texas*

I couldn't discern it above the noise of my engine, but reporters said "a reverent hush fell over the crowd." This was appropriate, for I was praying.

> *Lieutenant Benjamin D. Foulois, pilot of the first military flight in U.S. history, San Antonio, 1910*

I left New York yesterday morning headed for California, but I got mixed up in the clouds and must have flown the wrong way.

> *Douglas "Wrong Way" Corrigan, of Galveston and San Antonio, explains how he "inadvertently" flew across the Atlantic Ocean to Ireland, 1938*

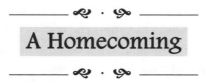

A Homecoming

As soon as it was light enough for us to see we went into the house, and the first thing we saw was the hogs running out. Father's bookcase lay on the ground, broken open, his books, medicines, and other things scattered on the ground, and the hogs sleeping on them. When Mrs. M——'s children, sister, and I got to the door, there was one big hog that would not go out till father shot at him.

Dilue Rose Harris, age ten, comes back to the family farm near Harrisburg after the Runaway Scrape, 1836

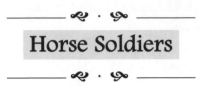

Horse Soldiers

The commissary and forage house were in a tolerable state of preservation, but the quarters and hospital were roofless and most of the woodwork had been removed. The village adjacent to the fort had been a station of the overland mail route, and when it was occupied by settlers and the fort filled with troops I have no doubt it was, as I was informed it had been, the prettiest frontier post in Texas, but now desolation reigned supreme. Sand, sand everywhere; dead buffalo lying on the parade ground, a few ancient rats and bats looked on us with an evil eye for disturbing their repose, and my first night's rest in the old commissary was broken by visions of old infantry sentinels stalking ghost-like on their beat, and the wind howling through the broken roof.

In Five Years a Cavalryman, or Sketches of Regular Army Life on the Texas Frontier, *H. H. McConnell of the 6th U.S. Cavalry describes conditions at Fort Belknap when it was re-occupied after the Civil War, 1867*

5:15	Reveille	1:00	Dinner Call
5:30	Assembly and Stable Call	1:30	Fatigue Call
6:30	Surgeon's Call	4:00	Stable Call
7:00	Breakfast	4:30	Recall
8:30	General Fatigue Call	5:30	First Call for Dress Parade
9:00	General Mount	6:00	To Arms

9:30	Battery Drill	8:00	Tattoo
10:30	Recall	8:15	Taps
12:00	First Sergeants and Water Call		

A sample of the bugle calls in a typical long day at Fort Richardson, 1869

He was a fighting man. He believed it was more important for the troops to scout the frontier and perform military duty than it was to build chicken coops for officers and interfere with the citizens of the country; and within two years after he took command, the occupation of the Indians was gone, the lives of the settlers were safe, and the early abandonment of numerous military stations possible, they being no longer needed.

> *Former Sergeant H. H. McConnell on the legacy of Colonel Ranald McKenzie and his 4th Cavalry, assigned to Fort Richardson in 1871*

Fort Bliss seemed to be the very antithesis of its name. I met with several officers who looked worn and melancholy. There was not the slightest suggestion of the "loved soldier boy" in their manners or their movements. They yawned and complained of the station, cursed the bad water and inveighed against the sandstorms. They longed for action and would much prefer the roughest kind of frontier service to the torrid tranquility of Fort Bliss.

> Chicago Times *reporter John F. Finerty, 1879*

The custom that obtains throughout the army of each officer selecting according to his rank the quarters which he may prefer, was never more fully enforced than at Fort Clark. Fifty times, perhaps, there was a general move of at least ten families, because some officer had arrived who, in selecting a house, caused a dozen other officers to move, for each in turn chose the one then occupied by the next lower in rank. We used to call it "bricks fall-ing," because each toppled that next in order over; but the annoyance was endured with great good nature.

> *Frances Boyd, wife of Captain Orsemus Boyd, on the peck-ing order for quarters at Fort Clark in the early 1870s, in* Cavalry Life in Tent and Field, *1894*

Huddled Masses

A man can make his living to his liking, and more independent than the Autocrat of Russia, or the Emperor of Austria. I would not exchange my fifteen acre lot, with the house on it, and the garden around it, near the city of Houston for all the thrones and heredi-tary dominions of both those noted persons.

> *Lewis A. Levy urges fellow Jews to emigrate from Europe to Texas in the* New York Asmonean, *1850*

Although Texas is the finest state in the union, and may be liter-ally regarded as a "land flowing with milk and honey," it is necessary to FIRST MILK THE COWS and GATHER THE HONEY, before they can enjoy either the one or the other, for nei-ther of them can be obtained without the aid of labor. Therefore, those who arrive here under an impression that they are to realize a fortune without working will soon find out that Texas is not the country that they supposed it to be.

> *Advice to immigrants from Jacob de Cordova, in* Texas: Her Resources and Her Public Men, *1858*

Dem Ersten Tod, dem Zweiten Not, dem Dritten Brot [For the first generation, death; for the second, want; for the third, bread]
> *Proverb among German immigrants of the mid-nineteenth century*

Whether traveling or at home, we had no peace, not even the church was free of their antics. In many instances it might have been just horseplay, but it had serious effects on the victims. These cowboys entered the church during the services with their hats on and smoking cigarettes. They would come around the altar during the Mass and curiously examine the contents of the chalice. One of them wanted to ride into the church on horseback and see how many targets he could score on the walls. On the road they would shoot at the Polander's feet, in many instances wounding him. A woman, caught alone on the road, was found with a knife-stab in her back. These and many other calamities we endured. As a protection against such and against the snakes that crawled everywhere, I provided myself with a revolver. With a rosary in my pocket and the revolver hanging in a scabbard on my saddle I went along that everyone who did not believe the word of God would believe my revolver—the God of the Americans.
> *Father Adolf Bakanowski, the spiritual head of the Polish colony of Panna Maria, on their relations with neighboring ranch hands, 1866*

If you see anybody about to start to Texas to live, especially to this part, if you will take your scalpyouler and sever the jugular vein, cut the brachiopod artery and hamstring him, after he knows what you have done for him he will rise and call you blessed. This country is a silent but eloquent refutation of Bob Ingersoll's [the Great Agnostic] theory; a man here gets prematurely insane, melancholy and unreliable and finally dies of lead poisoning.
> *William Sydney Porter (O. Henry), letter, 1884*

If You Can't Say Something Nice

In character and customs, the people are lazy, dissipated, with relative luxury in their dress, arms, and horses, pusillanimous, captious, and sarcastic murmurers, all stemming from the fact that the population of this province was formed from among the vagabonds and malefactors of the others.

Félix María Calleja del Rey, sent by the Viceroy of Mexico on a tour of inspection, is not taken with the inhabitants of New Spain's province of Nuevo Santander, which included what is now the region of Texas between the Nueces River and the Rio Grande, 1795

General Lamar may mean well—I am not disposed to impugn his motives—he has fine belles-lettres talents, and is an elegant writer. But his mind is altogether of a dreamy, poetic order, a sort of political troubadour and crusader, and wholly unfit by habit or education for the active duties and the every-day realities of his present station. Texas is too small for a man of such wild, visionary "vaulting ambition."

Anson Jones, 1839

Ima, you are not pretty. You will never be pretty, and you must never let anyone tell you so.

Ima Hogg's Aunt Fannie does her best to ensure that Governor Hogg's thirteen-year-old daughter doesn't get too full of herself, 1895

Indigenous Fauna

Of all the insects of Texas, the most disgusting and venomous creature is that species of spider called the tarantula. It grows enormously large—measuring, when expanded, five and six inches—and some say that it is even much larger than this. Its bite is considered more fatal than that of the rattlesnake, and is declared by many and generally believed to be without a remedy. It is, at any rate, a most malignant and disgusting insect [actually an inoffensive arachnid].

    Mary Austin Holley, Texas, *1836*

The fleas were as thick as the sands of the sea. Our clothes were actually bloody, and our bodies freckled after a night of warfare with the Vermine. And the Rats, I cannot convey an idea of the multitude of Rats in Houston at that time. They were almost as large as Prairie dogs and when night came on, the streets and Houses were litterly alive with these animals. Such running and squealling throughout the night, to say nothing of the fear of losing a toe or your nose, if you chanced to fall asleep, created such an apprehension that together with the attention that had to be given our other Companions made sleep well nigh impossible.

    C. C. Cox, "Reminiscences," 1902, on Houston in 1837

Wild Pigeons.—Large flocks of these birds have been wheeling and circling above us the last few days, seeking roosts and food. They make a noise in their passing like the rushing of a heavy wind, and there is a degree of grandeur in the regularity and rapidity of their movements, combined with the immensity of their number. They have made one roost about ten miles from town, and some of our neighbors went out and got some. Knocking down pigeons, netting partridges which are in immense numbers, and hunting buffalo which range within fifty miles of town are three sources of amusement which would be considered great in most settled countries.

Clarksville Northern Standard, *1843*

A few days out from Corpus Christi the immense herd of wild horses that ranged at that time between the Nueces and the Rio Grande was seen directly in advance of the head of the column and but a few miles off. The column halted for a rest, and a number of officers, myself among them, rode out two or three miles to see the extent of the herd. As far as the eye could reach to our right, the herd extended. To the left it extended equally. There was no estimating the animals in it. I have no idea that they could all have been corralled in the State of Rhode Island or Delaware, at one time.

In his 1885 Memoirs, *ex-President Ulysses S. Grant recalls sighting a mustang herd while a lieutenant in Zachary Taylor's army, 1846*

To be sure, quite a few beasts of prey are found here. There are panthers (a kind of tiger the size of a dog but shaped like a cat), bears, wolves, foxes, opossums, skunks, several types of snakes, and alligators in the lakes and rivers. But there is enough food for all the animals so they do not need to attack human beings. Snakes can be a nuisance and they crawl clear up to the second story, especially a type called the chicken snake because it eats chickens and eggs which it swallows whole. The reason for its intrusion into houses is that the hens usually have their nests under the beds and up in the lofts.

Elise Woerenskjold, who emigrated from Norway to Van Zandt County in 1847

I was at a loss to conceive why it should ever have been called "prairie dog." It is a very timid animal; but, when irritated, bites severely, as one of our young gentlemen can testify. It is but little larger than the gray squirrel, of a reddish brown color, with head, teeth, and feet, very similar to that animal, and a more appropriate name, in my opinion, would be "prairie squirrel."

Captain Randolph B. Marcy, 1849

Everybody has seen horned frogs. You see them in jars in the windows of apothecaries. You are entreated to purchase them by loafing boys on the levee at New Orleans. They have been neatly soldered up in soda boxes and mailed by young gentlemen in Texas to fair ones in the old States. The fair ones receive the neat package from the post office, are delighted with the prospect of a daguerreotype—perhaps jewelry—open the package eagerly, and faint as the frog in excellent health hops out, upon them. A horned frog is, simply, a very harmless frog with very portentous horns; it has horns because everything in its region—trees, shrubs, grass even has horns—and nature made it in keeping with all around it. A menagerie would not be expensive. They are content to live upon air and can live, I am told, for several months without even that.

Anonymous, "Animals and Things in Texas," 1853

My rattlesnake, my only pet, is dead. He grew sick and would not eat his frogs and died.

Lieutenant Colonel R. E. Lee, Camp Cooper, in a letter to his wife, Mary, in Virginia, 1856

We have fortunately passed the *jigger* district and their bites are healing. I wish I knew what was the real word—chigger or jigger—our boys pronounce it the latter. It is so small as to be almost invisible but soon builds a large bloody house about him which itches extremely, and if scratched is inflamed into a large running sore. Many cannot resist bringing them to this—though I have. But such a scratching goes on in tents as to annoy those who otherwise could sleep.

> *Artist Miner K. Kellogg, journal, 1872*

A skunk passed my ambulance and Count shot it after Peters failed, and ran up to dispatch it with a stick, accompanied by Loew, and both were perfumed *intensely* thereby—to the amusement of witnesses but to my disgust as Count is in my mess, and his perfumed jacket will drive me or him out of it. The camp odor is now unbearable—but as we are to move today this can be borne—the jackets of Count & Doctor Loew are however to be with us—to our constant disgust.

> *In his journal of a geological survey, painter Miner K. Kellogg records yet another instance of folly from the Austro-Hungarian Count Crenneville, a young seeker of adventure from Vienna, 1872*

One of the greatest curiosities ever open to the free gaze of the San Antonio public, was an armadillo, which was hauled about the streets yesterday on a countryman's wagon. The man found the animal while cutting wood in Atascosa county, and brought it in with the intention of selling it to some curiosity seeker... The specimen brought to this city yesterday was the first ever found in Western Texas, so far as we know of.

> San Antonio Express, *1879*

He was provokingly slow in comprehending the existence and nature of the dangers that threatened his life, and, like the stupid brute that he was, would very often stand quietly and see two or three score, or even a hundred, of his relations and companions shot down before his eyes, with no other feeling than one of stupid wonder and curiosity. Neither the noise nor smoke of the still-hunter's rifle, the falling, struggling, nor the final death of his companions conveyed to his mind the idea of a danger to be fled from, and so the herd stood still and allowed the still-hunter to slaughter its members at will.

> *William T. Hornaday,* The Extermination of the American Bison, *1889*

Mr. Louis Ledbetter of the Wanderers Creek Valley neighborhood was attending to some business matters in Quanah the other day. He says wolves were never more plentiful in his section than they are at the present time, and that they are having great sport running them with hounds.

> Quanah Tribune, *1896*

The rats. Golly, there were so many of them that at one time, that summer of 1926, the Rig Theater offered a bounty on rat tails. For ten or twelve rat tails, you could get admission into the theater.

> *Reminiscence of W. Horace Hickox, an oil worker in Borger during the boom years*

No wild animal, or domestic either, has as many vocal tones as the Longhorn. In comparison, the bulls and cows of highly bred varieties of cattle are voiceless. The cow of the Longhorns has one *moo* for her newborn calf, another for it when it is older, one to tell it to come to her side and another to tell it to stay hidden in the tall grass. Moved by amatory feelings, she has a low audible breath of yearning. In anger she can run a gamut. If her calf has died or been otherwise taken from her, she seems to be turning her insides out into long, sharp, agonizing bawls. I have heard steers make similar sounds. They seemed to be in the utmost agony of expressing something so poignant to them that the utterance meant more than life and would be willingly paid for by death.

J. Frank Dobie, The Longhorns, *1941*

Two factors have determined the precarious status of the big [ivory-billed] woodpeckers. The most obvious is the disappearance of the virgin woodlands upon which they depend. Almost as fateful, however, is the bird's size and striking appearance. With its overall body length of twenty-one inches (compared to the sparrow hawk at eleven, the broad-winged hawk at eighteen, the duck hawk at nineteen, the chicken hawk at twenty inches) and flamboyant black, white and red markings, it has evoked such awestruck names as "goodgod," "mygod," "godamighty." It has also evoked the pride of backwoods marksmen, who have made it a favorite target.

Doctor Pete Gunter, The Big Thicket: A Challenge for Conservation, *1971*

There are alligators in the Big Thicket too. For certain there is at least one, which escaped its pen in the Alabama and Coushatta reservation in the spring of 1970 and meandered down into Big Sandy Creek. I am sure many of the Indians would have liked to go with it, to get away from the tourists.

Doctor Pete Gunter, The Big Thicket: A Challenge for Conservation, *1971*

Indigenous Flora

It is impossible to imagine the beauty of a Texas prairie when, in the vernal season, its rich luxuriant herbage, adorned with its thousand flowers of every size and hue, seems to realize the vision of a terrestrial paradise... The delicate, the gay and gaudy, are intermingled with delightful confusion, and these fanciful *bouquets* of fairy Nature borrow tenfold charms when associated with the smooth verdant carpet of modest green which mantles around them.

> *Mary Austin Holley,* Texas, *1836*

The prairie in which I now found myself presented the appearance of a perfect flower garden with scarcely a square foot of green to be seen. The most variegated carpet of flowers I ever beheld lay unrolled before me—red, yellow, violet, blue, every color, every tint was there—millions of the most magnificent prairie roses, tube-roses, dahlias, and fifty other kinds of flowers. The finest artificial garden in the world would sink into insignificance when compared with this parterre of nature's own planting.

> *Charles Sealsfield (pseudonym of secretive German traveler Karl Postl),* Spirit of the Times, *1843*

Here were six or eight good species of wild grapes, several of which had not been seen by me previously. I had found my grape paradise! Surely now, thought I, "this is the place for experimentation with grapes!"

> *Thomas V. Munson, 1876 (who later rescued the French wine industry with grafts of Bell County mustang grapes, for which France presented him the Legion of Honor)*

An hour's ride had carried us from the hills to a wide valley that lay between the mountain ranges. That hour transported us from one vegetable world to another, as if we were in the hands of the genie of some New World Aladdin's lamp. The sparse mountain oaks and junipers, with their stunted and dwarfed bodies, had disappeared, and we were now among the inhabitants of the valley—or "flat" as it is termed by our unpoetic frontiersmen—a floral people even more stunted and dwarfed and of forms infinitely more strange and grotesque than their kin of the mountains. We had left a people of Quakers wearing the garments of peace and harmony; we had come among a people of war, frozen by some magic with sword in hand and armor buckled for the fray. Lance or sword or dagger peeped out from almost every bush, and where we saw a shrub without weapons in sight we scrutinized it with strong suspicion that somewhere in its drab or russett bosom there lurked some secret deadly missile ready to be thrust into the rash intruder.

And here stands the gatún, the robber baron, with curved claws thrust out from his castle; claws that never loosen once fastened, that grasp meat or raiment regardless of distinction, for everything is prey that comes his way.

Over there is the tasajillo, an Italian brave, hiding under cover at the street corner, eager to thrust his stiletto into his unsuspecting victim, ready as he does so to draw back into obscurity.

> *Judge Oscar Waldo Williams anthropomorphizes the plant life of the Chisos Mountains in Big Bend country, 1902*

Lupinus Texensis and any other variety of bluebonnet not heretofore recorded

> *Definition of the bluebonnet, according to the state legislature, 1971*

By far the most puzzling case of anomalous distribution which I have run across is the claim made in the 1930's by a biologist who had engaged in the original biological survey to have found three plants in the Big Thicket whose only other known occurrence at that time was in Iceland. The biologist is now long deceased, and efforts to discover which plants he referred to have been futile. It is possible that the claim is valid, but until someone can come up with definite evidence one can only file the puzzle under the "unsolved" heading. The ecological ties between Iceland and the Big Thicket certainly seem tenuous enough. On the other hand, one never knows about the Thicket.

> *Doctor Pete Gunter,* The Big Thicket: A Challenge for Conservation, *1971*

The founding of the National Wildflower Research Center was my way of repaying some of the debt for the delight and sustenance Nature has given me all my life.

> *Lady Bird Johnson explains what moved her to create the wildflower center which opened in Austin on her seventieth birthday in 1982.*

The Iron Horse

I was between Hearne and Bryan when I saw my first railroad train. We were all watching the laying of tracks. I was riding my pony the day I saw the train. I heard the terrible puffing and blowing noise and it frightened me and my horse. He squattered as if to make a wild jump and run away. I put the quirt on him and got him away from the scene as fast as I could. The train burned wood in the engine and traveled about twenty miles per hour, one engine did not pull over twenty cars. I can remember when the passenger trains did not run on Sunday as people in those days did not believe in desecrating the Sabbath by riding on a train.

> *R. C. Allen of Hearne remembers when the Houston & Texas Central Railroad came to Hearne in 1868.*

A freight train was leaving Amarillo traveling a few miles west of town, when Engineer King was instantly killed, and the fireman and brakeman badly used up. The sad calamity was due to a washout. The north bound passenger train had passed on a short time before. No blame can be attached to the management of the road, for in a sudden rainfall as of last Monday the rain will pour down in torrents and streaks, it may not be one hundred yards away. Such sudden and peculiar rain storms are one of the penances of the Panhandle.

> Amarillo Champion, *1888*

It was customary for one man to do the washing for the whole crew. We usually settled this by cutting the cards or a little game of "freeze-out" if time permitted. But it was surprising how little laundry is necessary when no ladies are present.

> *Clay Stevenson, working on the Rock Island line as it laid track across the Panhandle, 1901*

Mr. F. S. Hastings

Stamford, Texas

Dear Sir: 6:30 this morning in going to the Stockyards to feed at this place another train run into my stock train. On an open switch killed 2 cows & the rest of the cows in another car is feeling sore & some of them only got one horn left. The crew of both trains jumped off & myself. so it was no one hurt. 8 or 10 of the Kansas cowboys is out all over Town picking up our Cattle—wish you could see them coming down the street driving one or two of them cows—I think they got about 10 of the cows in a Pen (down in Town) & they heard of 5 cows in a corn-field just a little while ago, so I guess they will get most of them back today. I will leave here about 5 P.M. will make tomorrow market.

P.S. The Sheriff shot one cow on the street just a little while ago.

P.S. The cows down in town is making the horses run off with buggys and running all the women out of town.

P.S. The Rail Road they gives me a poor and sorry run.

P.S. They run my cattle 40 hours before this happened without feed. (how about that.)

> *Letter from an SMS cowhand named Dock to Frank Hastings, manager of the SMS Ranch, explaining a fiasco on the train ride north, 1917*

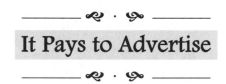

It Pays to Advertise

Walking, not long since, near the machinery of a mill, I was caught and carried between the cog-wheels and every bone in my body broken to pieces. A phial of *Ramrod's Tincture of Gridiron* being thrown into the pond, I found myself restored, and as whole and sound as a roach.

> Telegraph and Texas Register, *1838*

THE UNDERSIGNED has just received and opened for sale, the following articles, comprising the best stock of groceries ever brought to this place.

Old Rye, Monongahela and Corn
Whiskey, Champagne, Cognac,
Peach, American, and French Brandy.
Holland Gin, American,
Jamaica and New England Rum.
Port Madeira, Teneriffe, Claret, Muscat,
Sweet and Dry Malaga Wines, Wine Cherries.
A superior article of old Port and Madeira.
Brandy Cherries, Cordials and Syrups.
Porter & Ale, Wine & Cider Vinegar.
Pickled Lobsters, Sardines, Smoked
and Pickled Herrings, Choice Pickles,
Strawberry Preserves, Dried Fruit,
Pilot Bread, French Biscuit,
Sugar Crackers, Boston Crackers
and Soda Crackers.
Raisins, Rock and other Candies, Almonds,
Sugar, Coffee, Tea, Chocolate, Molasses
and Salt, Flour and Rice, Tobacco
of various qualities, Cigars,
Fine cut smoking Tobacco
and Pipes, Spices,
Loaf Sugar,
Black & Cayenne Pepper, Mustard,
Dye Stuffs of all kinds,
Starch, Blacking, Sulphur,
Shoe Thread, Percussion Caps,
Castor Oil, Turpentine, Crockery
Ware, Glass Ware, Wooden buckets, Tubs,
Rope, Bed Cord & Plough Lines, Powder,
Lead & Shot, Wax & Sperm
Candles, Window Glass,
Nails, Shaving Soap & Bar Soap,

Fire Crackers, Foolscap & Letter Paper.
GILBERT RAGIN.
A grocery bonanza in Clarksville, Northern Standard, *1845*

Secure the Shadow, ere the Substance fade.
>   *Slogan of the Allen and Whitfield Daguerrian Gallery, Houston, 1850*

Dr. Decle, who has recently located in San Antonio and established himself permanently, sent us a short time since a box of his "vegetable tooth powder" and a small bottle of "elixir antispasmodique et philodontique" which is to be used in connection with the powder as a tooth-wash. This preparation by Dr. Decle has received the encomiums of the Faculty of Medicine of Paris, and is doubtless very valuable, while the elixir is so pleasant. The Doctor is prepared to supply a limited demand.
>   San Antonio Herald, *1866*

A MALE AND FEMALE
HIGH SCHOOL
under the combined tutorship of
S. W. T. Lanham and Wife
Will open in the town of Weatherford on
Monday 22nd day of June.

Our past experience as Teachers warrants a confidence in our ability to give satisfaction in the advancement of students, and general scholastic system. We expect to merit a share of the public patronage, and respectfully solicit a trial. We have located here with the intention to remain and establish a permanent school.

RATES OF TUITION

Primary class, per month, specie,	$2.00
Intermediate, per month, specie,	2.50

First, per month, specie,	3.00
Latin, etc., per month, specie,	4.00

Students charged from admission to close of session except in case of protracted illness. Session to last 20 weeks.

Weatherford, June 20th, '68

Notice by future governor Sam Lanham and his wife Sarah, 1868

Within this hive we're all alive.
Good whisky makes us funny;
So if you're dry, come in and try
The flavor of our honey.

Bee Hive Saloon, Fort Griffin, 1870s

A WOMAN'S DREAM
She Sat Alone

In the moonlight, her beautiful cheek resting upon her hand, so soft and white and dimpled. You could tell, as you looked at her, that her thoughts were far away, and that she was thinking of something beautiful. Her eyes were wistful, the dimples in her cheeks had died out, and only the dimple in her chin remained, that little rosy cleft, the impress of Love's finger. She was less glowing than at times, but none the less lovely. I thought to myself, as I looked at her, that she was nearer to heaven than we coarser mortals, and I longed to know whither her pure heart turned itself. I approached her; she did not hear me. I spoke; she did not answer. I touched her softly on the arm, she looked up and smiled, a far-away smile, such as an angel might have given. "You are thinking very intently," I said. She answered, "Yes, I am thinking of SANGER BRO'S, who owing to the Removal of their Stock, and the want of room to exhibit their great quantity of Goods, are determined to reduce their stock at great sacrifice."

Handbill for Sanger Brothers department store, Dallas, 1873

THE JERSEY LILY
SALOON   COURT HOUSE
Judge Roy Bean—The Law West of the Pecos
Justice of the Peace   Whiskey Wine and Beer
Painted on the walls of Judge Roy Bean's courthouse in Langtry

GRAND-WINDSOR
HOTEL
Corner Main, Austin and Commerce Streets
Dallas Texas
The only first-class house in the city
Rates, $2, $2.50 and $3 per day; rooms and accommodations govern prices
Finest Sample Rooms in the State

The House recently has undergone changes, which in appointments and furnishing, none surpasses it. The Cuisine is now under the care of Col. John W. Ross. His superior in this department is not in the State. Capacity of House, 300 persons.
W. H. Whitla, Manager.
Dallas, 1886

The ladies of Mason, bless their sweet lives,
The radiant maidens and the good queenly wives
Dress finer than any who dwell in the West
Because Smith and Geistweidt sell them the best.
Mason News, *1889*

Dr. William's Pink Pills for Pale People contain all the elements necessary to give new life and richness to the blood and restore shattered nerves. They are an unfailing specific for such diseases as locomotor ataxia, partial paralysis, St. Vitus' dance, sciatica, rheumatism, neuralgia, nervous headache, the after effect of la grippe, palpitation of the heart, pale and sallow complexions and all forms of weakness either in male or female. They may be had of all druggists, or direct from the Dr. Williams Medicine Company, Schenectady, N.Y., for 50¢ per box, or six boxes for $2.50.

> Quanah Tribune, *1895*

I have bought an interest in the Wigwam Saloon, and you who, whether in El Paso or elsewhere, that admire pluck, that desire fairplay, are cordially invited to call at the Wigwam where you will have everything done to make it pleasant for you. All are especially invited to our blowout on the 4th.

> *Notorious gunman John Wesley Hardin in the* El Paso Times, *1895, three months before he was shot and killed by John Selman, possibly because Selman thought Hardin owed him some of the money he had instead invested in the Wigwam*

Neiman-Marcus Co. Cordially Invite You to Attend the Formal Opening of the New and Exclusive Shopping Place for Fashionable Women, Devoted to the Selling of Ready-to-Wear Apparel

> *The first advertisement for Neiman-Marcus, in the* Dallas Morning News, *1907*

Yesterday, Today, and Forever
We Back the Public Schools, the American Home, the
Protestant Church, the Constitution and Laws of the Land.
KU KLUX KLAN
Gainesville Klan No. 151
Realm of Texas
*Full-page advertisement in the Dougherty Memorial High
School yearbook, Gainesville, 1924*

REWARD
FIVE THOUSAND DOLLARS FOR DEAD BANK ROBBERS
NOT ONE CENT FOR LIVE ONES
*Incentive offered by the Texas Bankers' Association, 1928,
which led to eight murders of "robbers" for the reward*

Whiskey, $1.00 a gallon
Good Whiskey, $1.50 a gallon
Sign in a Big Thicket general store

River Oaks makes no pretension to exclusiveness. It is a friendly
neighborhood. And yet River Oaks attracts only the sort of people
who make good neighbors. It is a neighborhood in which the people you like, like to live.
*1934 advertisement for what is now the most exclusive neigh-
borhood in Houston*

If you've got it, flaunt it!
Slogan of Dallas-based Braniff Airways, 1960s

───── ❧ · ❧ ─────

Last Words and Epitaphs

───── ❧ · ❧ ─────

Thus perished our wise conductor, constant in adversity, intrepid, generous, engaging, adroit, skillful, and capable of anything.

Father Anastase Douay, member of the La Salle expedition, on the murder of La Salle by his own men, 1685

You know I never yet was caught unarmed by Indian or wild beast. I am a rude man and know not whom I may meet in another world. I wish to be prepared, as usual, *for all enemies.*

James B. "Brit" Bailey, 1832, requesting that he be buried upright, with his rifle at hand

How will things end in Texas? As God wishes them to end.

Mexican General Manuel de Mier y Terán, shortly before falling on his sword, depressed by the ascendancy of Santa Anna and the growing Anglo domination of Texas, 1832

Well, gentlemen. In eight days, liberty and home!

Reassurance from Colonel Juan José Holsinger to Fannin's men, soon to be slaughtered at Goliad, 1836

Me no Alamo! Me no Goliad!

Mexican soldiers at San Jacinto, 1836

Texas recognized. Archer told me. Did you see it in the papers?

Stephen F. Austin, dying words, 1836

I stay. I am an old man. I die here.

> *Cherokee Chief Bowles, killed at the Battle of the Neches, 1839*

I do not fear death but dread the idea of ending my life in a loathsome dungeon. Tell them I prefer a Roman's death to the ignominy of perpetual imprisonment, and that my last wish is for my country's welfare.

> *Philip Dimmitt, before committing suicide in a Mexican prison, 1841*

It is the effect of an oversensitive mind. I had neither money to bring my wife to this country nor to enable me to visit her.

> *George Childress, explaining to his doctor why he fatally stabbed himself six times with a Bowie knife, 1841*

Boys, I told you so; I never in my life failed to draw a prize.

> *Major James D. Cocke, after drawing the first fatal black bean in the Salado "decimation," 1843*

I see worlds upon worlds rolling in space. Oh it is wonderful.

> *Mary Austin Holley, last words, 1846*

I can die at Georgetown with fewer regrets than any place I know of.

> *Robert Jones Rivers, deathbed jest, 1854*

Rest in Peace
General
An old negro
Servant.
Property of
W. K. & S. E.
Pierce
Headstone, Cooke County

The cause of his death was a gun shot wound on the fore part of his head, inflicted by himself.
> *Findings of coroner's jury in the suicide of Thomas Jefferson Rusk, 1857*

Texas... Texas... Margaret...
> *Sam Houston, last words, 1863*

O pray for the soldier, you kindhearted stranger;
He has roamed the prairie for many a year;
He has kept the Comanches away from your ranches—
And followed them far over the Texas frontier.
> *On the stone at Fort Clark marking the grave of Private Peter Corrigan, Company D, 4th U.S. Cavalry, killed in an engagement with Kickapoo Indians, 1873*

You think you have done well... But you will not live long. I will see to that.
> *Prophet and medicine man Maman-ti to Kiowa chief Kicking Bird, reviled for his perceived collaboration with the U.S. Army, 1875 (Later that year Kicking Bird died, supposedly poisoned.)*

When I give the word, fire at my heart...

FIRE!

Más arriba, cabrones! [Higher up, you bastards!]
> *John Atkinson, to the firing squad of an El Paso mob (who ignored his request and shot him in the stomach, before giving him the* coup de grâce *with a pistol round in the head), 1877*

The world is bobbing around.
> *Outlaw Sam Bass, 1878 (on his 27th birthday)*

A brave man reposes in death here.
Why was he not true?
> *Headstone of Sam Bass*

Well, I haven't got much to say. I have got to die. I see a good many enemies out there, and only a mighty few friends. I hope to God you will forgive me; I will you. I hate to die, of course; any man hates to die, but I have learned this by taking the lives of men who loved life as well as I do. If I have any friends here I hope they will do nothing to avenge my death; if they want to avenge my death, let them pray for me. I deserve this fate. It's a debt I owe for my wild, reckless life. When it is paid, it will all be over. I hope you will forgive me; I will forgive you; whether you do or not, may God forgive me. I have nothing more to say.
> *Outlaw and murderer Wild Bill Longley, about to be hanged, Giddings, 1878*

Tumble-down Angel Tries to Climb Golden Stairs
> *Headline of a story of a prostitute's suicide,* Fort Worth Daily Democrat, *1880*

Four sixes to beat, Henry.
> *Deadly gunfighter John Wesley Hardin, rolling dice in the Acme Saloon seconds before John Selman gunned him down from behind, El Paso, 1895*

You know I am not afraid of any man, but I never drew my gun.
> *John Selman, after Deputy U.S. Marshal George W. Scarborough shot him four times "in self-defense" outside the Wigwam Saloon, El Paso, 1896*

Well, I feel like a new man, and I guess I am one.
> *Former Governor Sul Ross, who died five minutes later, poisoned by a biscuit accidentally made from flour that contained rat poison, 1898*

Well, I am just going to tell him that I have helped some and I have skinned some. Those I skinned could afford it, and those I helped needed it maybe.
> *Gambler Nat Kramer, when asked if he was prepared to face Saint Peter, Fort Worth, 1905*

In a recent nocturnal voyage on the watery waves of despair, I drifted over the vortex of eternity, but was wafted back by the breath of Fate. In this sensational journey I forgot neither my God nor my State. To Him I stood ready and willing to render a final account, with no fear of the Great Beyond.
> *Former Governor James S. Hogg, not long before his death in Houston in 1906*

Lawrence Sullivan "Sul" Ross, in an oil portrait
long after his days as a Texas Ranger.

The UT Institute of Texan Cultures at San Antonio
No. 68-243 Texas State Capitol Rotunda

Resting here until day breaks and darkness disappears is Quanah Parker, the last chief of the Comanche. Died Feb. 21, 1911, Age 64 years.

> *Headstone of Quanah Parker, son of Cynthia Ann Parker*

No man in the wrong can stand up against a fellow that's in the right and keeps on a-comin'.

> *Motto of Ranger Bill McDonald, engraved on his tombstone, 1918*

There are those who argue that everything breaks even in this old dump of a world of ours. I suppose these ginks who argue that way hold that because the rich man gets ice in the summer and the poor man gets it in the winter things are breaking even for both. Maybe so, but I'll swear that I can't see it that way.

> *Bartholomew "Bat" Masterson, last words, 1921*

Life's race well run
Life's work well done
Life's victory won
Now cometh rest

> *Epitaph of Governors Jim and Ma Ferguson*

As the flowers are made sweeter by the sunshine and dew,
So this old world is made brighter by the likes of you.

> *Inscribed on headstone of outlaw Bonnie Parker, 1934*

Death Wins Argument With Pitchfork Smith

> Dallas Morning News *obituary of notoriously combative writer William Bascom "Pitchfork" Smith, 1939*

What are you trying to do, burn up our port?

> *Swede Sandberg, vice president of the Texas City Railway, to longshoreman Pete Suderman, on the docks next to the freighter SS* Grandcamp, *moments before the ship's cargo exploded and destroyed most of Texas City, 1947*

You sure can't say Dallas doesn't love you, Mr. President.

> *Nellie Connally to President John F. Kennedy, November 22, 1963*

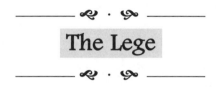

The Lege

If any member is too drunk to rise from his seat to speak, the chair shall appoint a committee of three to hold him up; but provided the member shall be dead drunk, and unable to speak, the chair shall appoint an additional committee of two to speak for him; provided, however, that if the member is able to hold up by tables, chairs, etc., then, and in that case, one of the committee shall gesticulate for him.

> *Rules of order for the incoming Texas Congress (including representatives from "Screamersville, Slizzlegig County, Screw-Auger Creek, Toenail, Epidemic, Hyena Hollow, and Raccoon's Ford"), proposed by the* Austin Daily Bulletin, *1841*

I have seen similar bodies at the North; the Federal Congress; and the Parliament of Great Britain, in both its branches, on occasions of great moment; but none of them commanded my involuntary respect for their simple manly dignity and trustworthiness for the duties that engaged them, more than the General Assembly of Texas. There was honest eloquency displayed at every opportunity for its use, and business was carried on with great rapidity, but with complete parliamentary regularity, and all desirable gentlemanly decorum. One gentleman, in a state of intoxication, attempted to address the house (but that happens elsewhere) and he was quietly persuaded to retire.

> *Frederick Law Olmsted,* A Journey Through Texas, *1857*

Members. I just want you to consider one thing. As many of you know, by the time I was twenty I had been a paratrooper for three years. And I swear this to you: If that man walks through those doors, it will be. Over. My. Dead. Body.

> *Representative Bill Kugle voices his opposition to a proposal to invite Senator Joe McCarthy to address the State Legislature, 1953*

The Texas Legislature consists of 181 people who meet for 140 days once every two years. This catastrophe has now occurred sixty-three times.

> *Molly Ivins, "Inside the Austin Fun House,"* Molly Ivins Can't Say That, Can She?, *1991*

The definitive statement on Texas political ethics—source unknown, but often quoted by Texas liberals—is: "If you can't take their money, drink their whiskey, screw their women, and vote against 'em anyway, you don't belong in the Legislature."

> *Molly Ivins, "Sleazy Riders,"* Nothin' But Good Times Ahead, *1993*

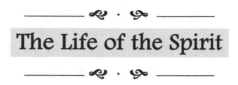

The Life of the Spirit

In truth if we had not taken note of the fact that the Son of God in His gospel does not command us to convert, but only to preach, and that according to the Apostle the work of conversion is not that of the one who plants nor of the one who waters, but only of God, who gives the increase, it would have been an intolerable toil of forty years.

> *Father Simón Hierro looks for some consolation in the failure of the missions in remote northeastern Texas, 1762*

The new county will never be the same again. Some of the ruffians of Robertson County had all hell scared out of them. Never have I heard such preaching and I'm sure no one else has.

> *Harrison Owen to Francis Slauter after Methodist preachers harangued hundreds of settlers at a camp meeting near Franklin, 1841*

A Mr. E. Cohen, lately from England, having a son born, concluded with a praiseworthy courage to perform the circumcision *himself*, as we have no *Mohel* nearer than New Orleans. People endeavored to persuade him to wait till the child could be taken thither, or a *mohel* be sent for. But he replied, that our Father Abraham performed this duty on the eighth day, why should he not do it also? He therefore did as he contemplated, in the presence of a surgeon, and the child is doing well.

> *The* Philadelphia Occident *reports on a do-it-yourself* bris *in Galveston, 1852*

L. W. Daly, buried Glenwood Cemetery, Dec. 13, 1876. Cause of death—Spiritualism.
> *Enigmatic entry from the records kept by Reverend Julyan Clemens, rector of Christ Church, Houston*

I believe that a sixth of the children I baptized died before reaching the light of reason, which means that I have 1,077 little angels praying for me.
> *Father Jean Baptiste Brétault, a missionary in Texas from 1872 to 1908*

Church-goers complain that the devotions at St. Mary's church are greatly interrupted on Sunday morning by the ten-pin alley at Turner hall. They think that one hour's cessation of hostilities would not be a great hardship.
> San Antonio Express, *1884*

Ah! what do we know of the beyond? We know that death comes, and we return no more to our world of trouble and care—but where do we go? Are there lands where no traveler has been? A chaos—perhaps where no human foot has trod—perhaps Bastrop—perhaps New Jersey. Who knows? Where do people go who are in McDade? Do they go where they have to fare worse? They cannot go where they have worse fare.
> *William Sydney Porter (O. Henry), letter, 1885*

The foreman [Colonel A. G. Boyce] of the XIT [ranch] introduced a strange practice; last Sunday he announced that six days were enough in every seven for man or beast to work, and that hereafter the XIT would observe Sunday.
> Tascosa Pioneer, *1888*

Religion does not seem to afford the Mexican much joy or comfort. He goes through it, however, as one gets his teeth repaired—not for the delicious thrill of joy lurking in the thing itself, but as a precautionary measure and as an evidence of his powers of endurance.

San Antonio Express, *1891*

The editor was reading a report of the regular meeting of the Dallas Pastors' Association, at which the Second Coming of Christ was learnedly considered. Dr. Seasholes declared that all good people will rise into the air, like so many larks, to meet the Lord and conduct him to earth—with flying banners and a brass-band, I suppose—where he will reign a thousand years. At the conclusion of this felicitous period Satan is to be loosed for a little season, and after he has pawed up the gravel with his long toe-nails and given us a preliminary touch of Purgatory, we are to have the genuine pyrotechnics.

William Cowper Brann, The Iconoclast

I haven't much use for gold-plated godliness. Christ never built a church, or asked for a vacation on full pay—never. He indulged in no political harangues—never told his parishioners how to vote—never posed as a professional Prohibitionist. He didn't try to reform the fallen women of Jerusalem by turning them over to the police, a la Parkhurst. Although gladiatorial shows were common in his country—and that without gloves—he didn't go raging up and down the earth like some of our Texas dominies, demanding that these awful crimes against civilization should cease. There is no record of his engineering a boycott against business men who dissented from his doctrine. I think he could have read a copy of the *Iconoclast* with far more patience than some of his successors.

William Cowper Brann, The Iconoclast

Prepare these priests for death.

> *Bishop Nicholas Gallagher to Father James Kirwin, expecting Saint Mary's Cathedral to collapse around them in the 1900 Galveston hurricane*

I can never do anything with this congregation as long as that face [the stained glass memorial to a former pastor] is looking down at me. This whole thing will have to burn down before I can do anything.

> *Fundamentalist preacher J. Frank Norris, five days before the First Baptist Church of Fort Worth, of which he was pastor, was in fact destroyed by fire, 1912 (Norris was tried for arson but acquitted, and he led the First Baptist until he died in 1952.)*

The Rev. Dr. J. Frank Norris, photographed in San Antonio in 1926, with twenty-six years yet to preside as pastor of the First Baptist Church of Fort Worth.

The UT Institute of Texan Cultures at San Antonio
No. 0098-L The San Antonio Light Collection

Someone has said that no one could look into the firmament and be an infidel. People who just go out and look up at the stars at night do not see them, they just see a few, but the cowboys see them and love them and with the old-timers they were guide and clock and almanac. Sometimes when you think things are all wrong, and that maybe you have been forgotten, get out somewhere with your cot and spend a night with the stars. After a while they will begin to come out in hundreds and thousands as though God were counting his angels and when you fall asleep there will be quiet and rest in your heart, and no matter what the sorrow, you will be ready to face it in the morning.

Frank Hastings, SMS Ranch Booklet, *1919*

I mean no offense to Matthew, Mark, Luke, and John, but when I was a kid if you would have asked me who invented Jesus, I would have looked around the congregation in the Salt of the Earth Church and answered, "The women." They seemed to enjoy Him more than the men. All allusion to Jesus, in sermon or song, prayer or testimonial, brought such tears to their eyes and such exaltations, "Oh, sweet Jesus!" that I came to suspect that women, to fill their need to have some object upon which to emote, had brought forth Christ and had had Him crucified, resurrected, and sent to Heaven—the full martyrdom with a Cecil B. De Mille ending—all for a good cry.

Bill Porterfield, A Loose Herd of Texans, *1978*

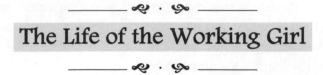

The Life of the Working Girl

On one side [of the Rio Grande at El Paso] an American woman known as the Great Western kept a hotel. She was very tall, large, and well made. She had the reputation of being something of the roughest fighter on the Río Grande, and was approached in a polite, if not humble manner by all of us, the writer in particular.

> *Legendary ranger "Rip" Ford meets legendary innkeeper, laundress, madam, and harlot Sarah Bowman in El Paso, 1849*

I poured out a drink and says to myself—"Don't look like we're going to have much fun here," and I threw my head back fer to swallow—and I NEVER GOT THAT DRINK. No one ever got their first drink in the Two Minnies. When I threw my head back to dreen the poison I seen the ceiling was glass, and there was anyways Forty girls walking around up there—NAKID as a jaybird, playing ten pins.

> *Tom Blevins's first experience of the Two Minnies saloon, Fort Worth, 1873*

Last Friday night a fire broke out in Mollie McCabe's "Place of Beautiful Sin." She owned the building which was entirely consumed, together with her household goods and clothes. The fire was caused by one of the damsels of spotted virtue.

> Jacksboro Frontier Echo, *1875*

Nearly all the bawdy houses in the city will give Christmas dinners to their "guests" and have issued printed invitations, sending them to nearly every young man in the city.

San Antonio Light, *1886*

Several young men have been in the habit lately of buying reserved seats in the opera house and presenting them to prostitutes. It is bad enough for them to buy the seats for these women at all, but it is a thousand times worse when they take advantage of the management to purchase seats in parts of the house where they know full well these women are not allowed to sit. Several prostitutes occupied such seats on the night of "Charley's Aunt," and the managers are anxious for the public to understand how it occurred, and to know exactly where the blame should rest. Fallen women are not allowed in any seats in the opera house except from the third dress circle row back, and in the gallery. And if they impose upon the management again as they have been doing, they will have to occupy the gallery or not enter the house. And further than this, the name of the person who buys tickets for them in the wrong part of the house will be published.

El Paso Times, *1894*

I've been anxious to visit Tillie. She is the talk of the border. Jim said he'd introduce me, so we went down there. It is a regular saloon, and a sort of hotel and dance hall combined; but Tillie makes the place different. She is tall, and I imagine she doesn't need those artificial bosoms the ladies are using now; hers look natural enough—I'll ask her when I know her better.

Ranger Alonzo Oden's diary entry after his long-awaited meeting with Tillie Howard, a famous El Paso madam in the 1890s

Clio Haskell was fined $200 for keeping a disorderly house and [Judge] George B. Hall took occasion to notify her that he would prosecute her for all violations from now on and her doctors will have to get busy to save her.

> *Lillian Kilcoyne, aka Clio Haskell, Greenville's leading madam, makes headlines again in the* Greenville Messenger, *1906 (Weeks later she sold out and cheerfully reopened in Terrell.)*

We find that under the existing conditions bawdy houses and bawds are promiscuously scattered throughout the city, greatly menacing the decent neighborhoods and offending decent and respectable communities and parts of the city. We feel that the measure hereby suggested by us will entirely eliminate such objectionable characters from the decent neighborhoods of the City.

> *Dallas city commissioners' report, 1910, recommending that prostitution be legalized in a designated sector known as "Frogtown"*

One chicken, one screw.

> *Fee schedule during the Depression, when cash was scarcer than poultry, at the brothel near La Grange run by Miss Jessie Williams, known thenceforth as the Chicken Ranch*

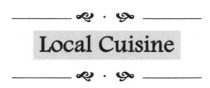

Local Cuisine

Corn is the most common crop and cornmeal is generally used for baking. It is well-liked by those who are used to it, but I must say frankly that I find it to be a poor type of bread.

Elise Woerenskjold, who emigrated from Norway to Van Zandt County in 1847

Children forgot—many of them had never known—what wheaten bread was like. Old Martin Varner used to tell a good story of his little son's first experience with a biscuit. The old man had managed to get together money or pelts enough to buy a barrel of flour. Mrs. Varner made a batch of biscuits, which, considering the resources of the country, were doubtless heavy as lead and hard as wood. When they were done Mrs. Varner set them on the table. The boy looked at them curiously, helped himself to one, and made for the door with it. In a few minutes he came back for another. Doubting the child's ability to eat it so quickly, the old man followed him to see what disposition he made of the second. The ingenious youngster had conceived a novel and not altogether illogical idea of their utility. He had punched holes through the center, inserted an axle, and triumphantly displayed a miniature Mexican cart. And I assure you, from my recollection of those pioneer biscuits, they were capable of sustaining a pretty heavy load.

Noah Smithwick recalls some daunting baked goods from pioneer days in The Evolution of a State, *1899*

We gathered the heads growing in the middle of the mescal plant. This had the color and almost the shape of a white cabbage head. A hole was dug, a fire built in it, and, after the whole cavity had been heated, the coals and ashes removed. The bottom was lined with cactus leaves, from which the thorns had been burned. The mescal was deposited and covered by cactus leaves; a layer of dirt was placed over them, and a fire built on top of all. It should have been kept burning all night. We judged it had been allowed to wane; the mescal was not properly cooked the next morning. We ate it nearly half raw. The writer was in the possession of a first-class appetite. He could not eat horse meat. It tasted like a sweaty saddle blanket smells at the end of a day's ride. The liver had an offensive smell; by holding his nose he forced down some of that strong-scented viand. He made a hearty breakfast on mescal and, as a result, suffered from colic.

> *Ranger John Salmon "Rip" Ford, on the trail from Austin to El Paso, 1849*

De boys hunts wolves and painters and wild game like dat. Dere was lots of wild turkey and droves of wild prairie chicken. Dere was rabbits and squirrels and Indian puddin', make of cornmeal. It am real tasty. I cooks goose and pork and mutton and bear meat and beef and deer meat, den makes de fritters and pies and dumplin's. Sho' wish us had dat food now.

> *Silvia King, interviewed in the 1930s by the Federal Writers' Project of the WPA, recalls life as a slave in 1850s Texas*

At first chile was a hellish food for me, but now I almost can swallow it like a Mexican.

> *In a letter to his family in Germany, Ernst Kohlberg explains that Indians and drought are not the only hazards that immigrants have to cope with, 1876*

A small supply of buffalo meat was brought in by our neighbor, Mr. T. Briggs, yesterday, and disposed of readily by the market. Bison steak, juicy and delicious, is a rarity in these days even in the West. It used not to be thus.

> Tascosa Pioneer, *1886*

Ignorance of the details of their manufacture is necessary to the complete enjoyment of tamales.

> San Antonio Express, *1897*

Hoover Hog
> *Depression-era nickname for the armadillo*

Texas does not, like any other region, simply have indigenous dishes. It proclaims them. It congratulates you, on your arrival, at having escaped from the slop pails of the other 49 states.

> *Alistair Cooke,* The Americans, *1979*

To the goggling unbeliever [Texans] say—as people always say about their mangier dishes—"but it's just like chicken, only tenderer." Rattlesnake is, in fact, just like chicken, only tougher.

> *Alistair Cooke,* The Americans, *1979*

Lone Star Literature

Now, dear reader in bidding you adieu, I will say: should you not be pleased with the substance of this *book*, I've got nothing to say in defence, as I gave you the best I had in my little shop, but before you criticise it from a literary standpoint, bear in mind that the writer had fits until he was ten years of age, and hasn't fully recovered from the effects.

> *Charles A. Siringo,* A Texas Cowboy, *1885*

Charlie Siringo never pretends; he is as free from trying to make effects as any man who writes about himself can be. His ignorance of rhetoric and his indifference to what appeals to the public were aids to honesty. From the first form in which he set down his experiences until the final form, he remained uninfluenced by the feeling of most writers on the West that they must raise thunder over oceans of blood. He specialized in bad men, but their gunmanship is never theatrical. His style, especially his early style, cannot be called dignified, but it is informed with the innate dignity of honesty.

> *J. Frank Dobie, Introduction to Siringo's* A Texas Cowboy, *1950*

I am the first and only serious writer that Texas has produced. These young people may turn out to be first rate. The woods are swarming with writers. In all this ferment, we're bound to get some good ones. But so far I am the only one. If you can show me the others, I'll be glad to see them!

> *Katherine Anne Porter on her place in Texas literature, 1958*

The most telling evidence of the Texans' voracious appetite for reading about themselves is the fact that for more than a quarter of a century they have, in effect, subsidized their own publishing house. This is the Naylor Company, of San Antonio, which annually publishes some forty new titles, mostly by and about Texans. While the company has begun publishing Southwestern authors who are not Texans in the last few years, it is "still Texas-minded to the core," as an officer of the firm said recently, and there is not much in the Naylor list to contradict him; to wit, "When God Made Texas," "Early Days in Texas," "Texas in 1848," "Texas in the Confederacy," "Texas and the Fair Deal," "A Hundred Years of Comfort in Texas," "Those Texans," "Towering Texans," "Texans with Guns," "You Can Always Tell a Texan," "I Give You Texas," "My State: Texas," "Texas Lawyers," "Texas Wildcatters," "Texas Wild Flowers," "Texas-broke," "Texas—Proud and Loud," "Texas Treasure Chest," "Texas Rhythm and Other Poems," "Poet Laureates of Texas," "The New Texas Reader," "The Texas Democrat," "The Texas Indians," "Night Fishing in Texas," "Deer Hunting in Texas," "Texas Lion Hunter," "Cavaliers in Texas," "Turkeys in Texas," and enough others in this vein to satisfy everybody except, apparently, Texans.

John Bainbridge, The Super-Americans, *1961*

Take the novel out. Leave the wild food in.

Editor's advice to Euell Gibbons, after reading the manuscript that, with drastic changes, became Stalking the Wild Asparagus, *1962*

A viny, tangled prose would never do for a place so open; a place, to use Ross Calvin's phrase, where the sky determines so much. A lyricism appropriate to the Southwest needs to be as clean as a bleached bone and as well-spaced as trees on the llano. The elements still dominate here, and a spare, elemental language, with now and then a touch of elegance, will suffice.

Larry McMurtry, In A Narrow Grave, *1968*

They [Roy Bedichek, Walter Prescott Webb, and J. Frank Dobie] have had a whole book of eulogies but no elegy, and something rather sad has happened. Three men who disliked establishments have been made into an Establishment, posthumously, and local belle-letterists are hard at work seeing that their memories are potted, pickled, and preserved.

Larry McMurtry, In A Narrow Grave, *1968*

Quite a council was called to decide whether or not Buffalo creek runs into Red river or into the "Goo-al-pa," as represented on the map. A clean sheet of paper was produced, and the map drawn according to their directions. But the council being composed of old men, to whom great deference was paid, and a great discrepancy of opinion existing among them, like most celebrated politicians, they at length agreed to compromise, and represented all the rivers as running parallel, ad infinitum.

> *Lieutenant James W. Abert, mapping the Panhandle in 1845, consults some helpful Kiowas and learns the futility of cartography by committee*

Of all the various boundary proposals put forward, this one which was finally adopted drew the most inconvenient and illogical line. It gave Texas a shape as peculiar as a gerrymandered county.

Northward, the "panhandle" projected nearly, but not quite, to the southern boundary of Kansas, leaving room for the "no man's land" that later became the grotesque elongation of Oklahoma. The triangular extension westward, with El Paso at its furthest limit, belongs to the region of the high plains and is geographically, economically, and historically connected with southern New Mexico, yet the parallel of 32°, for no particular reason, throws this natural area into two political jurisdictions.

> *Historian Percy M. Baldwin on the curious origins of the famous Texas outline, 1930*

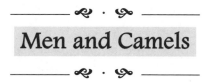

Men and Camels

I have the honor to report my arrival here with the camels. They are in good condition, considering their long confinement on shipboard and the tossing upon the sea that they have been subjected to and, with the exception of a few boils and swollen legs, are apparently in good health. On being landed and feeling once again the solid earth beneath them, they became excited to an almost uncontrollable degree, rearing, kicking, crying out, breaking halters and, by other fantastic tricks, demonstrating their enjoyment of the liberty of the soil.

> *Major Henry C. Wayne, delivering camels imported from Egypt for testing as an alternative to horses and mules for the Army, 1856*

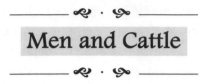

Men and Cattle

All goods in this part of the world are conveyed by means of ox wagons and you seldom see any other sort in this country. Ladies ride to meeting, come to town to trade etc in ox wagons and I have become a good ox driver from constantly hearing "Gee Berry, Wo, Come here Buck, Get up there Bell etc" and the way these fellows can crack their whips, twenty five and thirty feet long! You will never have the pleasure of hearing how loud a whip can be cracked until you come to Texas.

> *Alfred Howell, a young attorney newly settled in Greenville, in a letter to his brother in Richmond, Virginia, 1854*

There is an old army story to the effect that, when General Taylor's little army was on the march from Corpus Christi to Matamoras, a soldier on the flank of the column came upon and fired at a [longhorn] bull. The bull immediately charged, and the soldier, taking to his heels, ran into the column. The bull, undaunted by the numbers of enemies, charged headlong, scattering several regiments like chaff, and finally escaped unhurt, having demoralised and put to flight an army which a few days after covered itself with glory by victoriously encountering five times its numbers of human enemies.

> *Richard Irving Dodge,* The Hunting Grounds of the Great West, *1878*

Pleasant it was on a warm, clear night to circle slowly around a herd of cattle that were bedded down quiet and breathing deep and out there to catch the strains of song or fiddle coming from camp, where the fire was like a dim star. But it was pleasanter to be in camp and, while just catching now and then a note from singer or fiddler on herd, to be dropping off to sleep. As long as a cowboy heard music he knew that all was well.

> *Veteran cowboy John Young remembers the delights of music on the Chisholm Trail in the 1870s*

Boys, the secret of trailing cattle is never to let your herd know that they are under restraint. Let everything that is done be done voluntarily by the cattle. From the moment you let them off the bed ground in the morning until they are bedded at night, never let a cow take a step, except in the direction of its destination. In this manner you can loaf away the day, and cover from fifteen to twenty miles, and the herd in the mean time will enjoy all the freedom of an open range.

> *Trail boss Jim Flood, setting out from South Texas for Montana, 1882, as quoted by Andy Adams in* The Log of a Cowboy, *1903*

Any person caught monkeying with any of my cattle without permission will catch h__l.

> Yours in Christ,
> Grizzley Caleen

Tascosa Pioneer, *1886*

> Hence I say unto you, give the cowboy his due,
> And be kinder, my friends, to his folly;
> For he's generous and brave, though he may not behave
> Like your dudes, who are so melancholy.
> *William Lawrence Chittenden,* Ranch Verses, *1893*

Burch, Cartwright, Parks, Kilburn and Chancelor separated their calves from the cows last Saturday and we are all chuck full of such musics and wishing for a let up or some anodyne to produce sleep in the calves or ourselves, either one will be a relief.

> Canyon City Stayer *(motto: A Newspaper Devoted to Stock Raising), 1901*

It is remarkable that during my ten years on the trail I rarely ever had a man who would shirk his duty; had he been so inclined, he would have been ridiculed out of it. It is certain that no deadheads ever stayed in a cow camp any length of time.

> *Charles Goodnight, "Managing a Trail Herd"*

I am fully persuaded in my mind that we ought to own this bull—Like Ancient Briton [an 1893 champion Hereford], he stands out before America as the best—he has the reputation of a champion, and by all means should go to the champion herd. I believe that no one can afford to pay more for him than we can, mainly because the purchase of him will enhance the value of every whiteface we have. These facts will go down in the annals of history—Where is the champion bull of America in 1898, Sir Bredwell? On the Plains of Texas. Who owns them? C. C. Slaughter. To my mind, we had better pay ten times the value of this bull alone than to let him go to another herd.

> *Colonel Christopher Columbus Slaughter, founder of the Lazy S Ranch, to his son George, justifying his decision to purchase prize Hereford Sir Bredwell, 1899*

Cattleman and Colonel Christopher Columbus Slaughter

The UT Institute of Texan Cultures at San Antonio No. 80-440

When I was a small boy, my sister and I used to watch the big trail herds of cattle from the coast going north, and it seemed to me they would pass for hours. We were watching through the cracks of a ten-rail fence. These steers were from four to ten years old, coaster steers, big longhorns out of the brush. The men wore leather chaps and toe fenders over the stirrups and all of them carried rifles and pistols. Many of them carried them across the pommel of their saddle and not in a scabbard as we do today.

That was when I first got my idea that I wanted to be a cowboy.

> *Arch Sneed, a hand on the XIT ranch from 1902 to 1905 before he found a new career as an engineer on the Rock Island line*

The cowboy I saw on the curb of North Main Street that day looked remarkably like Tom Mix, with a good big jaw and an aquiline nose and even a hank of dark hair falling across his forehead from beneath a pushed-back Stetson. I knew what he was because in those departed, naïve days practically nobody but ranch hands and their employers wore boots and big hats in town, where it was generally felt that only they had the right. This cowboy was not, however, acting like the Tom Mix I'd known. He was unmistakably hog drunk, and was hanging onto an iron street-sign post with both hands while he vomited partly in the gutter and partly on himself, having recently, it appeared, ingested some chili with beans.

> *John Graves, introduction to* Cowboy Life on the Texas Plains, *1982*

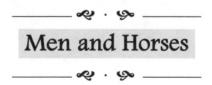

Men and Horses

Oh what mulish animals are mules! Many of these silly brutes, when they get their feet into sticky mud over the hoof, conclude they are mired and immediately fall down; and even when lifted up again they will not stand, but quietly permit themselves to be dragged out of the mud by the ears or tail; and even then it is sometimes necessary to strangle them to make them get up.

> *Josiah Gregg vents his frustrations to his diary after struggling to lead his mule train across what he christened "Quagmire Creek" in the Panhandle, 1840*

The lasso is usually from twenty to thirty feet long, very flexible, and composed of strips of twisted ox-hide. One end is fastened to the saddle, and the other, which forms a running noose, held in the hand of the hunter who thus equipped rides out into the prairie. When he discovers a troop of wild horses, he maneuvers to get to windward of them and then to approach as near as possible. If he is an experienced hand, the horses seldom or never escape him, and soon as he finds himself within twenty or thirty feet of them, he throws the noose with unerring aim over the neck of the one he has selected for his prey. This done, he turns his own horse sharp round, gives him the spur, and gallops away, dragging his unfortunate captive after him breathless and with his windpipe so compressed by the noose that he is unable to make the slightest resistance. After a few yards, the mustang falls headlong to the ground and lies motionless and almost lifeless, sometimes badly hurt or disabled. From this day forward, the horse which has been thus caught never forgets the lasso; the mere sight of it makes him tremble in every limb, and, however wild he may be, it is sufficient to show it to him or lay it on his neck to render him as tame and docile as a lamb.

> *Charles Sealsfield, "Adventures in Texas," from* Spirit of the Times, *1843*

THE WELL KNOWN THOROUGH BRED
HORSE TENNESSEEAN

Will stand until the 15th July evening, at his stable in the town of Clarksville and will be let to mares, at eight dollars the single leap, or Fifteen dollars the season, payable within the season, or Twenty-five dollars to insure; payment to be made when the fact is ascertained, or the mare traded.

Mares from a distance can be accommodated with pasture free of charge, or fed upon grain, at an underrate price.

Edward West
Clarksville Northern Standard, *1845*

I stood at street corners in waiting to see some ranchero, or farmer, emerge from a saloon and vault clean into the saddle of his patient mustang. This feat is thoroughly Texas, and should be seen to be appreciated.

A correspondent for Frank Leslie's Illustrated Newspaper, *reporting from Austin in 1880*

The horse breaker or "Bronc Buster" usually names horses as he breaks them; and if the horse has any flesh marks or distinct characteristics, it is apt to come out in the name, and any person familiar with the practice can often glance at a horse and guess his name. For instance, if he has peculiar black stripes toward the tail with a little white in the tail you are pretty safe to guess "Pole Cat." If his feet are big and look clumsy, "Puddin Foot" is a good first chance. The following names occur in three mounts, and to get the full list I had to dig hard, and both men left out several horses until I asked about them, because always the suspicion that something was going to be done that would take a horse: Red Hell, Tar Baby, Sail Away Brown, Big Henry, Streak, Brown Lina, Hammerhead, Lightning, Apron Face, Feathers, Panther, Chub, Dumb-bell, Rambler, Powder, Straight Edge, Scissors, Gold

Dollar, Silver City, Julius Caesar, Pop Corn, Talameslie, Louse Cage, Trinidad, Tater Slip, Cannonball, Big Enough, Lone Oak, Stocking, Pain, Grey Wonder, Rattler, White-man, Monkey Face, Snakey, Slippers, Jesse James, Buttermilk, Hop Ale, Barefoot, Tetoler, Lift Up, Pancho, Boll Weevil, Crawfish, Clabber, Few Brains, Show Boy, Rat Hash, Butterbeans, Cigarette, Bull Pup. Feminine names are often used, such as Sweetheart, Baby Mine, or some girl's name.

Frank S. Hastings, SMS Booklet, *1919*

I take better care of these horses than I do myself.

Shannon Davidson, winner of the Pony Express-style horse race from Nocona to San Francisco, 1939

Cowboys could perform terrible labors and endure bone-grinding hardships and yet consider themselves the chosen of the earth; and the grace that redeemed it all in their own estimation was the fact that they had gone a-horseback. They were riders, first and last. I have known cowboys broken in body and twisted in spirit, bruised by debt, failure, loneliness, disease and most of the other afflictions of man, but I have seldom known one who did not consider himself phenomenally blessed to have been a cowboy, or one who could not cancel half the miseries of existence by dwelling on the horses he had ridden, the comrades he had ridden them with, and the manly times he had had.

Larry McMurtry, In A Narrow Grave, *1968*

Years ago someone pointed out that Texas is hell on women and horses. He was wrong about horses, for most horses are considered to be valuable, and are treated well.

Larry McMurtry, In A Narrow Grave, *1968*

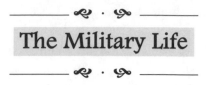

The Military Life

The drum is rattling; this is the signal for the calling of the roll. Most of the volunteers are gathered around the fire, roasting raw meat at the spit. Soon a few soldiers, half-dressed, stand in line before their sergeant who, list in hand, awaits the arrival of the others. The men are without their firearms; several hold in one hand a domestic looking wooden spit, hung with a piece of roast meat, in the other the famous Bowie knife. Quite a few volunteers have failed to take their place in the line, as the position of their meat over the fire or the stage it has reached in its cooking forbids even a temporary absence.

> *Prussian immigrant Herman Ehrenberg of the New Orleans Greys—a band of volunteers—describes the informal camp discipline at the siege of San Antonio, 1835 (Ehrenberg was one of the few Greys to escape the slaughter at Goliad a few months later.)*

While still in Natchitoches [Louisiana], I had decided to offer my services as an officer in the forthcoming war. I spoke about this to the Adjutant General of the Texas army who happened to be there and was informed that all of the government appointed positions had been filled and that the officers of the volunteer companies were elected by members of the corps.

At the election of officers, the choice was not for the most worthy, but for the one who could buy the most whiskey. It is no wonder, therefore, that orders were oftentimes not only ignored, but also laughed at; the captain commanded, and the soldier did as he pleased. I would have been glad to lead an armed group for the liberation of the land where I had sought to make my home, but under such existing conditions I would not and could not bear arms.

> *Friedrich W. von Wrede, a decorated Hessian officer and a*
> *veteran of Waterloo, passes up his opportunity to be the von*
> *Steuben of the Texas Revolution, at Nacogdoches in 1836*

I have been in more wars and fought less than any living man.

> *U.S. Congressman and Army Captain Thomas Terry*
> *Connally, lamenting the end of World War I before he could*
> *participate, just as he had missed action in the Span-*
> *ish-American War twenty years before*

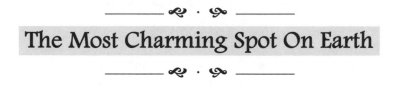

The Most Charming Spot On Earth

Within my knowledge, there is not a country of the same extent that has more poor land; that has a greater number of local causes of disease—that has more unseemly and disagreeable swamps and ponds, or that has more snakes, mosquitoes, ticks and flies than Texas.

> *James W. Parker,* The Rachel Plummer Narrative, *1844*

When we were upon the high table-land, a view presented itself as boundless as the ocean. Not a tree, shrub, or any other object, either animate or inanimate, relieved the dreary monotony of the prospect; it was a vast illimitable expanse of desert prairie—the dreaded "Llano Estacado" of New Mexico; or, in other words, the great Zahara of North America. It is a region almost as vast and trackless as the ocean—a land where no man, either savage or civilized, permanently abides; it spreads forth into a treeless, desolate waste of uninhabited solitude, which always has been, and must continue, uninhabited forever; even the savages dare not venture to cross it except at two or three places, where they know water can be found.

> *Captain Randolph B. Marcy, 1849*

Such a country as this I almost wish I had never seen it, if I had wings to fly I would abandon it forever, it is surely the last place on earth for a woman to live, or anyone else. I don't believe it was ever intended for civilized people, it was made for wild Indians and buffalo.

> *Susan Bartholomew, whose diaries recorded life on the frontier from 1865 to 1896 and provided material for the annual Fort Griffin Fandangle*

250 miles to the nearest Post Office, 100 miles to wood, 20 miles to water, and 6 inches to hell. God bless our home! Gone to live with the wife's folks.

> *Sign on an abandoned homestead, Blanco County, 1887*

Here there were no trees! Was hell just a place where no trees grew, no birds sang?...

Hell was a place where the winds blew all the time, winds that tormented you, but would not let you die...Winds that drove you *almost* crazy, but didn't let you know the relief that complete insanity would bring...Demon winds!...

> *Dorothy Scarborough, whose 1925 novel* The Wind *provoked scorn from die-hard Texans for its unflattering portrait of life in the Texas wilderness*

Le Mot Juste

It appeared to be the only study of some of our teamsters to invent the most blasphemous oaths; and the cool, slow, and decided manner in which the imprecations were uttered, showed that they wished all within their hearing to have the full benefit of their studies. I have heard swearing in many quarters, but for originality, deliberate utterance and deep wickedness, I have never heard that of some of the drivers on the Santa Fé Expedition equalled.

George Wilkins Kendall, Narrative of the Texan Santa Fe Expedition, *1844*

His [a drover's] conversation was upon horses, his clear voice ringing high above the noise of the car-wheels, as he laughingly recounted anecdotes of adventures on ranches in the West, nearly every third word being an oath. He caressingly cursed; he playfully damned; he cheerfully invoked all the evil spirits that be; he profaned the sacred name, dwelling on the syllables as if it were a pet transgression, and as if he feared that it would be too brief.

Edward King, The Great South, *1875*

We were joined by a youth who apparently had formed his idea of cowboys from dime novels. He aired his lungs by cussing everything from his cow pony to the minister we met in the road. His language was sulphuric, with a rich assortment of oaths. He seemed astonished that we did not try to compete with him.

Baylis John Fletcher, Up the Trail in '79

The Gibber gave us so many moments to remember. Both his tongue and his syntax regularly got so tangled that his language was dubbed Gibberish and provided the state with wonderful divertissement. He once closed a session by thanking the members for having extinguished theirselfs. Upon being reelected at the beginning of another session, he told members he was both grateful and "filled with humidity."

When anxious to press forward with legislations, he would urge members to "disperse with the objections." He once announced, "This is unparalyzed in the state's history." Other Gibberisms: "This legislation has far-reaching ramifistications." "It could have bad ramifistications in the hinterlands." "This problem is a two-headed sword: it could grow like a mushing room." "We don't want to skim the cream off the crop here." "We'll run it up the flagpole and see if anyone salutes that booger."

> *Molly Ivins on retiring House Speaker Gib Lewis, "Gibber and Other Misdemeanors,"* Nothin' But Good Times Ahead, *1993*

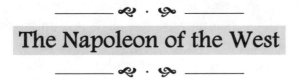

The Napoleon of the West

Up to this time I had enjoyed among my fellow-citizens a reputation which I preferred to that of being brave: that of being generous in victory. It was necessary, in order that my misfortune be complete, that even the only virtue that my most bitter enemies never denied me should now be questioned. I am made to appear more ferocious than a tiger, I, who in a country the most generous and humane, pride myself on being known for my clemency.

> *Antonio López de Santa Anna,* Manifesto, *1837*

Portrait of Antonio López de Santa Anna,
from a daguerroetype of about 1850.

The UT Institute of Texan Cultures at San Antonio No. 92-63

Nothing is more degrading or more fatal to justice than perfidy garbed in the raiments of truth.—Cicero

General Antonio López de Santa Anna has always appeared in this garb, and today, robed in the same mantle of duplicity, he comes before the whole nation—that nation which has bestowed upon him so many favors, so many distinctions, so much wealth—to deceive her as he has always done.

> *Rámon Martínez Caro (Santa Anna's former secretary),* A True Account of the First Texas Campaign, *1837*

Texans! The generous Mexican nation against which you have offended, as a reward to one of your number for benefits conferred, pardons you. In his name, which I love, I restore to you the liberty which you lost, while invading our territory, and violating our domestic firesides.

Go home and publish that the Mexican nation is as generous with the conquered, as it is valiant on the field of battle. You have experienced their courage; experience now their magnanimity.

> Mexico, June 13, 1842
> Antonio López de Santa Anna
> *Pardon of the Texans taken prisoner in the disastrous Santa Fé Expedition*

Neighbors

[Mrs. Bingham], a lady of much intelligence and good breeding, acknowledged that a change of residence to Texas had cost her a great struggle, but declared that she had since become quite reconciled to her abode, and does not feel that want of society which she apprehended. She has four or five children, and several neighbors around her, and can at any time, she remarked, pay a visit to a friend by taking a short ride of ten or twenty miles.

> *Anonymous,* A Visit to Texas in 1831

This is King Fisher's road. Take the other.
> *Sign at a fork in the road near the home of gunfighter King Fisher, 1870s*

I was coming out of the Castalon Country several years ago, and a fellow waved me down a few miles south of Alpine, Texas, and wanted to know if I knew Polk Hinson. I told him I did. He wanted to know where he lived. I told him that Polk lived in the first house on the left, down the road. He thanked me and started to drive off. He stopped and said, "By the way, how far is it?"

I said, "About a hundred miles."
> *C. M. "Buck" Newsome,* Shod With Iron, *1975*

The Nobility

Not long ago a little Duke who owes his title to the fact that his great-grand-aunt was the paramour of a half-wit prince, kindly condescended to marry an American girl to recoup his failing fortunes. A little French guy whose brains are worth about two cents a pound—for soap-grease—put up a Confederate-bond title for the highest bidder and was bought in like a hairless Mexican pup by an American plutocrat. Now half-a-dozen more little pauper princelings and decadent dukelings are trying to trade their worthless coronets for American cash. But the fact that many a man boasting of his American sovereignty will dicker with a titled young duke, instead of using the forecastle of a No. 9 foot to drive his spinal column up through his plug-hat like a presidential lightning-rod; will actually purchase for his daughter some disgusting little title upon which rests the fateful bar-sinister of a woman's shame, and is encumbered by a dizzy young dude, too lazy to work and too cowardly to steal—too everlastingly "ornery" to raise a respectable crop of wild oats—proves that the young lollipop lordlings haven't a monopoly of the Gall of the Globe.

William Cowper Brann, "Speaking of Gall"

Old-Timers

I reckon I have been shot at and missed more times than any man livin', but I wouldn't say so because nobody would believe me and I wouldn't blame them. There is so much hot air shot about the pioneer days. It's a big nuisance to be an old frontiersman.

Legendary rancher Charles Goodnight, interviewed in his twilight years by the Fort Worth Star-Telegram *in 1926*

Charles Goodnight looks like the archetype of the tough, successful cattle baron.

The University of Texas, Center for American History

A man has got to be at least seventy-five years old to be a real old cowhand. I started young and I am seventy-eight. Only a few of us are left now, and they are scattered from Texas to Canada. The rest have left the wagon and gone ahead across the big divide, looking for new range. I hope they find good water and plenty of grass. But wherever they are is where I want to go.

Teddy Blue (E.C. Abbott), We Pointed Them North*, 1939*

I never et much. I get up for breakfast, turn around for dinner, and go to bed for supper. When I was riding up the Chisholm Trail the range cooks sort of held it against me because I was a light-eating man. I've always drunk lots of coffee, chewed plenty of tobacco, and haven't tried to avoid any of this good Texas weather.

Walter Washington Williams of Franklin, reputedly the last surviving veteran of the Civil War, shares the secret to his longevity, 1949

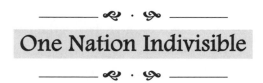

One Nation Indivisible

Whereas, the Government of the Mexican United States, have by repeated insults, treachery, and oppression, reduced the White and Red emigrants from the United States of North America, now living in the Province of Texas, within the Territory of the said Government, into which they have been deluded by promises solemnly made, and most basely broken, to the dreadful alternative of either submitting their freeborn necks to the yoke of an imbecile, faithless, and despotic government, miscalled a Republic; or of taking up arms in defence of their inalienable rights and asserting their Independence; They—viz.—the White emigrants now assembled in the Town of Nacogdoches, around the Independent Standard, on the one part, and the Red emigrants who have espoused the same Holy Cause, on the other, in order to prosecute more speedily and effectually the War of Independence, they have mutually undertaken, to a successful issue, and to bind themselves by the ligaments of reciprocal interests and obligations, have resolved to form a Treaty of Union, League and Confederation.

> *Preamble to the Fredonian Declaration of Independence, 1826*

There never was a more silly, wild, quicksotic scheme than that of Nacogdoches, and all sober, honest thinking people here view it in the same light.

> *Dr. John Sibley, Louisiana judge and politician, on the failed insurrection at Nacogdoches (the "Republic of Fredonia" lasted less than two months), 1827*

The Romans conceded lands to the tribes of the North and by so doing destroyed the foundation on which during many centuries they had built the most extensive empire that had ever governed the world.

> *Mexican cabinet, on the dispatch of General Manuel de Mier y Terán to assess rebellious feeling among Americans in Texas, 1827*

Man seeks happiness in the improvement of his condition. This is a natural and invariable law—a law that will bind Texas to Mexico with stronger ties than the force of large armies. With a due regard to this law and the true spirit of the system of government that rules the nation, no one could harbor a suspicion that Texas would ever secede.

> *Stephen F. Austin, August 1832*

The Republic of Texas has made known her desire to come into our Union, to form a part of our Confederacy and enjoy with us the blessings of liberty secured and guaranteed by our Constitution. Texas was once a part of our country, was unwisely ceded away to a foreign power, is now independent, and possesses an undoubted right to dispose of a part or the whole of her territory and to merge her sovereignty as a separate and independent state in ours. I congratulate my country that by an act of the late Congress of the United States the assent of this Government has been given to the reunion, and it only remains for the two countries to agree upon the terms to consummate an object so important to both.

> *President James K. Polk, inaugural address, 1845*

The final act in this great drama is now performed; the Republic of Texas is no more.

> *President Anson Jones, at the ceremony of annexation, Austin, 1846*

Anson Jones, the last President of the Republic of Texas.

The UT Institute of Texan Cultures at San Antonio No. 75-548

161

Sir:

Enclosed, I have the honor to submit the report of the State Lunatic Asylum, and commend the same to the consideration of your honorable body.

> *Governor Sam Houston, forwarding the ordinance of secession to the Senate, 1861*

The secession leaders...tell us if war comes that the superior courage of our people with their experience of the use of firearms, will enable us to triumph in battle over ten times our number of Northern forces. Never was a more false or absurd statement ever made by designing demagogues. I declare that Civil War is inevitable and near at hand. When it comes the descendants of the heroes of Lexington and Bunker Hill will be found equal in patriotism, courage and heroic endurance with the descendants of the heroes of Cowpens and Yorktown...When the tug of war comes, it will indeed be the Greek meeting Greek. Then, oh my fellow countrymen, the fearful conflict will fill our fair land with untold suffering, misfortune, and disaster.

> *Sam Houston, 1861*

We, the people of West Texas, acknowledging with gratitude the grace of God in permitting us to make choice of our form of Government, do ordain and establish this Constitution:

> *Preamble to the constitution of the proposed state of West Texas, 1869*

Only a Novel

Let him never touch a novel. They paint beauty more charming than nature, & describe happiness that never exists. They will teach him to sigh after that, which has no reality, to despise the little good that is granted us in this world, & to expect more than is ever given.

> *Lieutenant Colonel Robert E. Lee, writing home to his wife, Mary, in Virginia on the education of their son, 1856*

I wish [my sons] to be early taught an utter contempt for novels.
> *Sam Houston, last will, 1863*

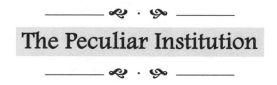

The Peculiar Institution

Article 30. After the publication of the law, there can be no sale or purchase of slaves which may be introduced into the empire. The children of slaves born in the empire shall be free at fourteen years of age.

> *From the Imperial Colonization Law, passed in Mexico in 1823*

Article 13. From and after the promulgation of this Constitution in the principal town of each District, no body can be born a slave, and the introduction of slaves under any pretext after six months from said publication is prohibited.

> *From the Constitution of the Mexican State of Coahuila y Texas, 1827*

All persons of color who were slaves for life previous to their emigration to Texas, and who are now held in bondage, shall remain in the like state of servitude, provided the said slave shall be the bona fide property of the person so holding the slave as aforesaid. Congress shall pass no laws to prohibit emigrants from the United States from bringing their slaves into the Republic with them, and holding them by the same tenure by which such slaves were held in the United States, nor shall Congress have power to emancipate slaves; nor shall any slave-holder be allowed to emancipate his or her slaves, without the consent of Congress, unless he or she shall send his or her slave or slaves without the limits of the Republic. No free person of African descent, either in whole or in part, shall be permitted to reside permanently in the Republic, without the consent of Congress; and the importation or admission of Africans or negroes into this Republic, excepting from the United States of America, is forever prohibited, and declared to be piracy.

> *General Provisions, Section 9, Constitution of the Republic of Texas, 1836*

If any person shall murder any slave, or so cruelly treat same as to cause death, the same shall be felony and punished as in other cases of murder.

> *Texas Legislature, 1840*

...had a devil of a rompuss with the negro woman Susan, after giving her a sound beating which she well deserved—she absquatolated to furrin parts.

From the diary of German immigrant Adolphus Sterne of Nacogdoches, a merchant and legislator, 1843

Marse Jones, he am awful good, but de overseer was de meanest man I ever knowed, a white man named Smith, what boasts 'bout how many slaves he done kilt. When Marse Jones seed me on de block, he say, "Dat's a whale of a woman." I's scairt and can't say nothin', 'cause I can't speak English. He buys some more slaves and dey chains us together and marches us up near La Grange, in Texas. Marse Jones done gone ahead and de overseer marches us. Dat was a awful time, 'cause us am all chained up and whatever one does us all has to do. If one drinks out of de stream we all drinks, and when one gets tired or sick, de rest has to drag and carry him. When us git to Texas, Marse Jones raise de debbil with dat white man what had us on de march. He git de doctor man and tell de cook to feed us and lets us rest up.

Silvia King, 100 years old more or less when interviewed in the 1930s, tells how she came to Texas as a slave about 1850

They are of all people on earth the most happy...I have never yet heard of a slave that committed suicide.

Sam Houston, Boston, 1855

NEGROES RAN AWAY

On last Monday night, four Negroes, a man, a woman, and two children—belonging to Maj. S. Peters who lives on Padre Island, ran away. It is supposed that they are working their way toward Mexico. Boys on the Río Grande, times are hard, and now you have a chance to get a large reward.

Corpus Christi Ranchero, *1861*

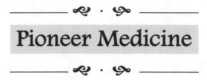

The remedy used by the Indians, when bitten [by a rattlesnake], is simple, ready at hand, and said to be effective. They kill the snake immediately, taking care at the same time that he does not bite himself; they then cut off his tail, and apply the fleshy part to the bite; after holding it an instant to the wound, they remove it and cut off another piece of the snake, about an inch long, and apply it; this is repeated until the whole snake is used up. The poison having a greater affinity for the flesh of the serpent, than for that of the man, is soon extracted, and the wound becomes perfectly harmless.

> *Mary Austin Holley,* Texas, *1836*

When first called to a patient, the charge for one visit shall be five dollars. After nine o'clock, P.M., the charges for professional visits shall be doubled in all cases. For visits out of the limits of the city, an extra charge of one dollar a mile during the day, and two dollars a mile at night.

> *Medical and Surgical Society of Houston, 1841*

In going through a thick chapparal today, my pony was bitten on the leg by a rattlesnake. An old hunter told me to chew up some tobacco and tie it on the wound, which I did and, except for a slight swelling, no bad results followed from the bite. (I have seen tobacco used frequently since as a remedy for the bite of a rattlesnake, and there is no doubt it is a good one but not equal to whiskey or brandy taken in large quantities.)

> *Bigfoot Wallace, 1871*

When a suspected person is found on the train going to Galveston, he is summarily seized at the muzzle of the six-shooter and tumbled off the train on the open prairie. If he is sick there is no shelter, no hospital, no bed, no preparation for medical treatment, no anything to keep him from dying like a dog. If he is well, there is no house, no food, no place where the necessities of life are to be had, and if he approaches a human residence he is driven off by an excited and fear stricken people armed with shot guns. Every house has its separate quarantine, any hamlet or village takes the responsibility of turning back trains, stopping the mails and disorganizing the commerce of an entire State. Human pity is extinguished, human mercy abolished, and insane panic armed with a shot gun rules supreme.

> Houston Daily Telegram, *on the effects of yellow fever on society, 1878*

Since I am recalling first impressions of a frontier garrison, I cannot omit the surgeon's first notable case, which could hardly have occurred elsewhere than in a tropical country. It was officially reported "a case of maggots in the nose." A soldier had fallen asleep in the sun, and during his unconscious half-hour a fly peculiar to the tropics deposited its larvae in his nostrils. It was only heroic treatment with chloroform that destroyed the maggots and saved the man from suffocation.

> *Recent bride Maria Brace Kimball and her army surgeon husband, James, just arrived at Fort Clark in 1892, encounter one of the more insidious hazards of life at a cavalry post.*

Oh, people didn't get sick before they built all these fine hospitals. We had a little camphor, soda, and vinegar; a tea made from green cocklebur leaves is good for snake bite. Oh, I was laid out for dead one time at Hackberry Grove, but they laid me in an ant bed, and when those ants went to work, I wasn't out long.

>*Jim Roark, longtime foreman of the Y Ranch, Foard County, recalls 1920s doctoring cowboy style*

Prairie Coal

To the Hon Commissioners Court of Sherman County, Texas

We the undersigned respectfully petition your Hon. body to secure fuel for the County Court House during the coming winter by employing citizens of the County to gather wood and "cowchips" in sufficient quantity to ensure the comfort of the County officers while engaged in the discharge of their various duties; the object of this petition being to furnish employment to citizens who need it, and to keep the money of the county within the county.

>*A request submitted by five civil servants in 1889 (which was denied)*

How true was the expression: "the windmill draws our water and the cows cut our wood." The lowly cowchips around which I at first tip-toed and raised my skirts held a place of high esteem.

>*Mary Blankenship discovers the prairie's most abundant form of fuel on her family's new homestead claim near Lubbock in 1902, in* The West Is for Us

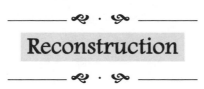

Reconstruction

I have too much regard for the memory of the brave men who died to preserve our government to authorize Confederate demonstrations over the remains of anyone who attempted to destroy it.

> *General Philip Sheridan, forbidding any public ceremony for General Albert Sidney Johnston, killed at Shiloh and being moved from New Orleans to Texas in 1867 (Thousands still turned out to pay their respects in Galveston, Houston, and Austin.)*

Mr. Pannell, they tell me you dislike to bury my soldiers.

General, whoever told you that told a damned lie. It's the pleasantest thing I've had to do in years. I would like to bury every damned one of you.

> *Houston sexton H. G. Pannell to the Reconstruction commandant in Houston, during the 1867 outbreak of yellow fever, which killed Federal occupation troops and ex-Rebels with impartial efficiency*

The *Huntsville Times* reports many of the most estimable wives and daughters, in that region, as doing all their domestic and housework.

> *The* Greenville Independent *deplores the hardships imposed by Reconstruction, 1868*

The Red Man

I felt no fear whatever from these neighbors, but would sleep with all our doors open, with twenty-five or thirty Indians within call. It was amusing to see them parade the streets of Mategorda with their long plaid, red, blue, garments, which I had made for them, the tails tipped with ornamental feathers. One of the young women learned to speak very good English; I dressed her in my clothes, and one day thought to have some fun with her, invited her to take tea with me. But the joke turned to my own expense, for she not only used her knife and fork properly but her cup, saucer and plate like it was an every day affair.

> *Mary Helm describes Indian relations in 1830s Matagorda in* Scraps of Early Texas History, *1884*

The Texians appear to have long forgotten they are human beings...As to the idea of ever civilizing them, it never enters the brain of the settler.

> *Francis C. Sheridan,* Galveston Island, *1840*

There was one Indian girl of a most queenly mien, and whose appearance I will assay to describe. Her forehead and nose were admirably Grecian; her form and limbs delicate and handsome; a graceful and flowing carriage, which, disdaining the Grecian hump or bow attitude, assumed the erect and stately figure of the forest pine; her step was scenic and proud; and her long, black hair, shining in the sun, fell in plaits to her girdle; her dress was a robe of richly dressed and ornamented skins, tastefully manufactured, falling below her knees, a scarf of the same material thrown in drapery over her shoulders, fringed and painted in no mean taste, with bead sandals, reaching beneath her robe. She stood and moved a native queen of the prairie, an imposing model of savage beauty.

> *Francis S. Latham,* Travels in the Republic of Texas, 1842

Jerusalem, captain, yonder comes a thousand Indians!

> *Ranger Noah Cheery, at the beginning of the battle at Walker's Creek, in which the Colt revolver first proved its worth, 1844*

Apache scalps are worth two hundred dollars, prisoners two hundred and fifty.

> *C. C. Cox reports the official bounties offered as a measure to counter Apache raiders, El Paso, 1849*

It was like clock-work—every time I raised my Colt's carbine, they stuck an arrow in me.

> *Jem Carr, Texas Ranger, wounded four times in a battle with Comanches, 1851*

I have not the least belief in the Noble Savage. I consider him a prodigious nuisance and an enormous superstition. His calling rum fire-water and me a pale-face, wholly fail to reconcile me to him. I call him a savage, and I call a savage a something highly desirable to be civilized off the face of the earth.

> *Frederick Law Olmsted,* A Journey Through Texas, *1857*

I have this day crossed all the Indians out of the heathen land of Texas and am now out of the land of the Philistines. If you want to have a full description of our Exodus out of Texas—Read the "Bible" where the children of Israel crossed the Red Sea. We have had about the same show, only our enemies did not follow us to R[ed] River. If they had—the Indians would have—in all probability sent them back without the interposition of Divine providence.

> *Major Robert S. Neighbors, in a letter to his wife, after reluctantly escorting peaceful Caddo, Tonkawa, and Anadarko Indians out of Texas to reservations north of the Red River, 1859*

Me Cincee Ann.

> *Cynthia Ann Parker, hearing her name after being recovered from Comanches in 1860, twenty-four years after her capture at age eleven*

If the Texans had kept out of my country, there might have been peace. But that which you now say we must live in, is too small. The Texans have taken away the places where the grass grew the thickest and the timber was the best. Had we kept that, we might have done the things you ask. But it is too late. The whites have the country which we loved, and we only wish to wander on the prairie until we die.

> *Comanche Chief Ten Bears, 1867*

I believe in making a tour of your frontier with a small escort, I ran the risk of my life; and I said what I now say to you, that I will not again voluntarily assume that risk in the interest of your frontier, that I believe Satanta and Big Tree will have their revenge if they have not already had it, and that if they are to have scalps, that yours is the first that should be taken.

> *General William Tecumseh Sherman to Governor Edmund Davis in 1873, expressing his disgust at the governor's parole of two chiefs sentenced to death for leading the 1871 Salt Creek Massacre*

The Kickapoo is a kind of perverted Indian; he is unlike the original tribes of Texas, who, like their neighbors in Mexico, were mild-mannered until aroused by ideas of wrong. He was born with the genius of murder and rapine firmly implanted in his breast, and being somewhat civilized, of course he is much worse than if he were a pure savage.

Edward King, The Great South, *1875*

Me love white man heap. Me been after Kiowa Indian. He steal me pony. Kiowa bad Indian; heap. Kiowa want me to help him fight white man. Me tell him no, me love white man. Me tell him Kiowa been a fool. Mebbe-so Kiowa kill one white man. Ten white men come and mebbe-so Kiowa kill ten white man. Mebbe-so Indians kill hundred white man. Me tell Kiowa then thousand white men come and kill every damn Kiowa! Indian can no stop white man. Mebbe-so Indian dam up Red River. Mebbe-so Red River stop running one day. Mebbe-so he stop running two days. Then water get up so big he wash Indian's dam all off.

Declaration by Pawnee, begging for beef from passing drovers, in Up the Trail in '79

Never ride upon a bowman's left; if you do, ten to one that he will pop an arrow through you. When mounted an Indian cannot use his bow against an object behind and to his right...

The bow is placed horizontally in shooting; a number of arrows are held in the left hand; the bow operates as a rest to the arrows. The distance—the curve the missile has to describe in reaching the object—is determined by the eye without taking aim. Arrows are sped after each other in rapid succession. At the distance of 60 yards and over, arrows can be dodged, if but one Indian shoots at you at one time. Under forty yards the six-shooter has little advantage over the bow. At long distances the angle of elevation is considerable. It requires a quick eye to see the arrow and judge the whereabouts of its descent, a good dodger to move out of the way, and a good rider withal to keep in the saddle. A man is required to keep both eyes engaged in a Indian fight.

> *Tactical advice from a veteran Indian fighter and ranger, in* Rip Ford's Texas, *1885*

The Karankawa Indians [were] a fierce tribe, whose hand was against every man. They lived mostly on fish and alligator with a man for fete days when they could catch one.

> *Noah Smithwick,* The Evolution of a State, *1899*

The boys held an inquest on the dead Indian and, deciding that the gunshot would have proved fatal, awarded me the scalp. I modestly waived my claim in favor of Rohrer, but he, generous soul, declared that, according to the rules of the chase, the man who brought down the game was entitled to the pelt, and himself scalped the savage, tying the loathsome trophy to my saddle...

> *Noah Smithwick,* The Evolution of a State, *1899*

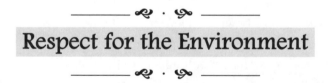

Respect for the Environment

Never have men so quickly and ruthlessly slashed a forest as they did the Southern pine forests. Labor was cheap, the country flat to gently rolling, the weather rarely severe. The Southern lumber baron pushed his "cut and get out" policy to an extreme not seen before or since. Oddly enough, very little lore resulted from this massive transformation. The lumberjack of the north and northwest has no counterpart in Texas mythology. Compared with the backwoods bear hunter, the cowboy, or the oilfield roughneck, the East Texas timber worker appears as drab a character as the Southern mill worker he in part resembles, tied to the region in which he, his wife, and children were born, constantly in debt to the company store.

> *Doctor Pete Gunter,* The Big Thicket: A Challenge for Conservation, *1971*

I think we are all willing to have a little bit of crud in our lungs and a full stomach rather than a whole lot of clean air and nothing to eat. And I don't want a bunch of environmentalists and communists telling me what's good for me and my family.

> *State Representative Billy Williams, who died of lung cancer in 1982*

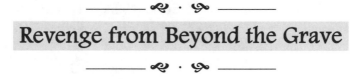

Revenge from Beyond the Grave

It is my will that $1,000.00 be put at interest of my means for ulterior purposes, to-wit: In view and in anticipation of Gordon Templeton committing some crime worthy of prosecution (of which he is so capable), that it shall be the duty of my said Executors to employ said interest and principal if necessary in employing lawyers to prosecute him, in all Civil matters where he may be sued and if there should be a case that would send him to the penitentiary or stretch his neck no means shall be withheld in prosecuting him to the death as he is a swindler, a liar, a scoundrel and a hipocrite and should my said Executors fail to do this my will in relation to Templeton then and in that case they shall forfeit all the interest they have in my said estate as above mentioned.

In a bizarre provision of his will, Matt Ward of Marion County provides for the perpetual badgering of a despised nephew, 1861

Riches Are for Spending

An old irishman by the name of "Hunky-dorey" Brown kept the store and did the settling up with the men. When he settled with me he laid all the money, in silver dollars, that I had earned since commencing work, which amounted to a few hundred dollars, out on the counter and then after eyeing me awhile, said: "Allen, Pool & Co. owe you three hundred dollars," or whatever the amount was, "and you owe Allen, Pool & Co. two hundred ninety-nine dollars and a quarter, which leaves you seventy-five cents." He then raked all but six bits into the money drawer.
   Charles A. Siringo, A Texas Cowboy, *1885*

I'm going to pay you but you'll have to be patient. I'll tell you my system. When I get my bills, I put them in the trash basket, and when I get my paycheck, I reach in there and pull out two bills. If you don't quit harassing me, I'm not going to put you in the basket.
   Young, struggling journalist Hubert Roussel works things out with the Houston Electric Company during the Great Depression

Raising money is easy—paying it back is what's hard.
   Dallas banker Robert L. Thornton, 1948

Some Texas millionaires—especially those who have had money for a generation or two—seem to suppress their natural desire to brag out loud and assume, instead, a tight-lipped smugness, which is apt to turn into a truculent uneasiness. Apparently unsure of recognition as a member of the peer group, they seem constantly on the verge of throwing aside their affected complacency, grabbing by the shoulders whoever they feel has not been properly impressed, and demanding, "Look here, don't you know who I am?"

John Bainbridge, The Super-Americans, *1961*

Money is like manure. If you spread it around, it does a lot of good, but if you pile it up in one place, it stinks like hell.

Financier Clint W. Murchison

People who know how much they're worth aren't usually worth that much.

Nelson Bunker Hunt, 1980

Little ol' boy in the Panhandle told me the other day you can still make a small fortune in agriculture. Problem is, you got to start with a large one.

Agricultural Commissioner Jim Hightower, 1986

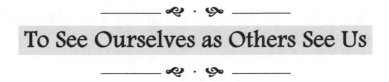

To See Ourselves as Others See Us

He who goes to Texas presuming on his own intelligence and their want of it, will find himself mistaken. I am acquainted with no community of the same number, which embodies more shrewd, intelligent men than that of the single star republic.

Thomas A. Morris, Miscellany, *1842*

I would here correct one erroneous impression in relation to the character of the early settlers of Texas. Many believe they were rude and ignorant, with many vices and few virtues, and for the most part refugees from justice and enemies to law and order. That there were some rude and illiterate people among them is no more than may be said of almost any society, and that some were vicious and depraved is equally true, but what there was of evil you saw on the surface, for there was no effort at concealment and no reason to act a borrowed part. Assassins, if there were any, appeared as such; now they often appear in the guise of gentlemen, that they may conceal their true characters and accomplish their object. No one estimates more highly than the writer, the intelligence, enterprise, and virtue of the present population, and yet he fully believes there were in the early history of Texas more college-bred men, in proportion to the population, than now, and as much intelligence, good common sense, and moral and religious culture among the females as among the ladies of the present day.

"T.J.P.," in A Texas Scrapbook, *D.W.C. Baker, 1875*

Non-Texas Americans find much in Texas to praise, but, adopting the traditional Old World attitude toward the New, they usually find much more to criticize. The faults of Texas, as they are recorded by most visitors, are scarcely unfamiliar, for they are the same ones that Europeans have been taxing us with for some three hundred years: boastfulness, cultural underdevelopment, materialism, and all the rest. In enough ways to make it interesting, Texas is a mirror in which Americans see themselves reflected, not life-sized but, as in a distorting mirror, bigger than life. They are not pleased by the image. Being unable to deny the likeness, they attempt to diminish it by making fun of it. As a consequence, Texas has become the butt of jokes too numerous—not to mention tedious—to count. Still, the image remains. In the end, perhaps, it may not be possible to escape the fact that the epitome of America is Texas, and the epitome of Texas is its most picturesque product, its millionaires.

John Bainbridge, The Super-Americans, *1961*

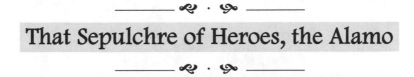

That Sepulchre of Heroes, the Alamo

I am besieged by a thousand or more Mexicans under Santa Anna. I have sustained a continued bombardment for twenty-four hours, and have not lost a man. The enemy have demanded a surrender at discretion; otherwise the garrison is to be put to the sword, if the place is taken. I have answered the summons with a cannon shot, and our flag still waves proudly from the walls. I shall never surrender or retreat!

Lt. Col. William B. Travis, at the Alamo, 1836

Remember the Alamo!

Sam Houston's army at San Jacinto, 1836

The Rev. Valdez desires to buy some stone from which is in the wall of the Alamo. The corporation of San Antonio agreed that there be sold him whatever he may need at four reals per cart load.

Minutes, San Antonio City Council, 1840

Lieutenant Colonel William Barret Travis, heroic commander at the Alamo.

Texas State Library and Archivew Commission

LAST FALL OF THE ALAMO

"I am—
Excuse me, I was—the Alamo.
Ye who have tears to shed,
Shed.
Shades of Crockett, Bowie and the rest
Who in my sacred blood-stained walls were slain!
Shades of the fifty or sixty solitary survivors,
Each of whom alone escaped;
And shades of the dozen or so daughters,
Sisters, cousins and aunts of the Alamo,
Protest!
Against this foul indignity.
Ain't there enough jobs in the city
That need whitewashing
Without jumping on me?
Did I stand off 5000 Mexicans in '36
To be kalomined and wall-papered
And fixed up with dados and pink mottoes
In '96?
Why don't you put bloomers on me at once,
And call me
The New Alamo?—
Tamaleville!
You make me tired.
I can stand a good deal yet,
So don't have any more chrysanthemum shows
In me.
If you do
I'll fall on you.
Sabe?"

> *William Sydney Porter mocks the commercial misuse of the Alamo,* Houston Post, *1896*

As the party is registering in the big visitor's book, the comfortable looking matron, who has heretofore not said much, takes a retrospective view of the Alamo's interior and remarks: "This is all very interesting and inspiring, but it is horribly damp and unhealthy in here. Even if those patriots hadn't been killed so cruelly, I dare say they would all have taken rheumatism and died anyway."

Tourists at the Alamo, San Antonio Express, *1897*

Sittin' and Spittin'

By exerting no undue energy and exercising a bit of consideration he could have expectorated *over* the rail.

> *Mrs. John Lockhart, on Sam Houston's spitting tobacco on her porch, 1842*

Some of the women chewed snuff without cessation, and such women neither "tucked" nor "inserted" [tucking muslin and inserting lace]. They simply rocked to-and-fro, and put in a word occasionally. It must be remembered that the majority of women who "dipped" had likely formed the habit when it was their only physical tranquilizer, through days and nights of terror, and pain, and watchfulness; and that the habit once formed is difficult to break, even if they desired to break it, which was not a common attitude.

> *English immigrant Amelia Barr (also author of* Remember the Alamo, *a novel), describes female society in Austin, where she lived in the 1850s and '60s, in her autobiography* All the Days of My Life, *1913*

Beau Monde wants a law making it a penitentiary offence for a man to expectorate tobacco juice on sidewalks and in streetcars. It is all well enough to talk of woman's suffrage, the Monroe Doctrine, the tariff and finance, but they are secondary issues when compared to the above. If the politicians want a real live issue let them rally around the standard of the anti-tobacco chewers' great American union for the suppression of public nuisances.

> *Alice Parsons Fitzgerald, editor of the Dallas society newspaper* Beau Monde, *1896*

Sodbusters

We have heard that the ranchman was antagonistic to the farmer, and will with force resist his approach. In other words, that the cowman with the aid of his cowboys and his carbine will be an obstacle and block civilization's path. This is but idle talk. Those who speak so are not adept in observational science. A little time and patience will show them in Texas the rough ranchman transferred and softened into the stock farmer and agriculturalist as naturally and as quietly as the Winter softens into Spring.

> *Colonel W. E. Hughes of the Mill Iron Ranch doesn't see what all the fuss is about, at the Cattlemen's Convention, Dallas, 1887*

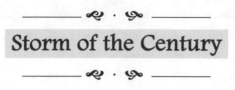

Storm of the Century

(see **Blue Northers** and **Texas Weather**)

The opinion held by some who are unacquainted with the actual conditions of things, that Galveston will at some time be seriously damaged by some such disturbance, is simply an absurd delusion.
Isaac M. Cline, head of the Galveston weather station, 1891

For eastern Texas: Rain Saturday, with high northerly winds, Sunday rain, followed by clearing.
The U.S. Weather Bureau forecast that appeared in the Galveston News *on Saturday morning, September 8, 1900*

The hurricane which visited Galveston Island on Saturday, September 8, 1900, was no doubt one of the most important meteorological events in the world's history. The ruin which it wrought beggars description, and conservative estimates place the loss of life at the appalling figure, 6,000.
Isaac M. Cline, U.S. Weather Bureau, in his official report on what is still the worst natural disaster ever to strike the United States

This here fire's been going on more than a month. To my knowledge, upwards of sixty bodies have been burned in it—to say nothing of dogs, cats, hens, and three cows. It takes a corpse several days to burn all up. I reckon there's a couple dozen of them—just bones, you know—down near the bottom. Yesterday we put seven on top of this pile, and by now they are only what you might call baked.

Fireman supervising a bonfire of the dead after the Galveston hurricane, 1900

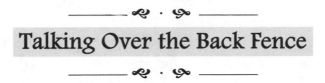

Talking Over the Back Fence

Mr. J. T. Holland has been laid up several days with a bad wound. While driving a nail it flew into his eye, cutting it seriously and the doctor is keeping him closely indoors at his ranch.

Sam Kersey says he sleighed his girl into the snow. Got upset, that's the sleigh, and there was a burying there, but he finally dug her out, that is the girl, and he found her smiling, the girl, and was glad, the boy, but did not make another engagement to ride. She wouldn't; had enough.

Felix Franklin says he knows no news. Being the first of the month, he is busy dodging bill collectors.

Amarillo News, *1895*

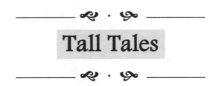

Tall Tales

While I was engaged in the conquest and pacification of the natives of this province, some Indians who were natives of other provinces beyond these had told me that in their country there were much larger villages and better houses than those of the natives of this country, and that they had lords who ruled them, who were served with dishes of gold, and other very magnificent things; and although, as I wrote Your Majesty, I did not believe it before I had set eyes on it, because it was the report of Indians and given for the most part by means of signs, yet as the report appeared to me to be very fine and that it was important that it should be investigated for Your Majesty's service, I determined to go and see it with the men I have here.

> *Francisco Vásquez Coronado, governor of Nueva Galicia, reports to King Carlos I of Spain why he set out across New Mexico and Texas to seek the imaginary treasures of Gran Quivira, 1541*

On the third day a party of about fifteen Indians appeared on the edge of the bluff, east of Adobe Walls Creek, and some of the boys suggested that I try the big "50" on them. The distance was not far from seven-eights of a mile. A number of exaggerated accounts have been written about this incident. I took careful aim and pulled the trigger. We saw an Indian fall from his horse. The others dashed out of sight behind a clump of timber. A few moments later two Indians ran quickly on foot to where the dead Indian lay, seized his body and scurried to cover. They had risked their lives, as we had frequently observed, to rescue a comrade who might be not only wounded but dead. I was admittedly a good marksman, yet this was what might be called a "scratch" [lucky] shot.

> *Hunter and scout Billy Dixon describes his legendary shot with a Sharps buffalo gun at the Second Battle of Adobe Walls, 1874, in* The Life and Adventures of "Billy" Dixon, *by his wife, Olive*

A Mr. Knight rode into Cleburne a few days ago on a horned horse. The animal was in every respect a well formed two-year-old colt except that it has two horns about 15 inches long growing from the top of its head. The curiosity is to be sold to a northern showman.

> Bastrop Advertiser, *1883*

Some fool started the report that a gang of Indians numbering about five hundred stampeded from the nation and struck Saulsbery [Salisbury] "all spradled out" and painted the town crimson by killing twenty odd persons and burning the town on last Thursday night. When the report first reached Canyon the people here gave it little credit, but as all kinds of blood-curdling reports kept coming in our people commenced to take things a little more serious, and when the stage driver arrived here Saturday at 10 A.M. he told the thing more scary than ever and said that reports reached Amarillo just before he left that the state rangers were fighting the Indians and that two or three of the rangers had been killed. He further said the redskins were making for the Tule and would very likely cross the canyons at this place. The story was then believed by all our citizens and they began to make ready to fight Indians...In the meanwhile Sheriff Wise and Jas. Patton were dispatched to Amarillo to find out anything they could in regard to the way the Indians were moving. They returned home about sun-down and reported the whole thing was a farce and not a word of truth in the report. Our citizens then stacked arms and once more breathed easy. Quite a number of men here took their wives and children to Amarillo. Everybody was badly scared and there is no use denying the fact. It is a strange thing how such reports can get out and carried so far without any foundation.

  Canyon City Echo, *1891*

About six o'clock this morning the early risers of Aurora were astonished at the sudden appearance of the airship which has been sailing through the country.

  It was traveling due north, and much nearer the earth than ever before. Evidently some of the machinery was out of order, for it was making a speed of only ten or twelve miles an hour and gradually getting toward the earth. It sailed directly over the public square, and when it reached the north part of town collided with the tower of Judge Proctor's windmill and went to pieces with a terrible explosion, scattering debris over several acres of ground, wrecking the windmill and water tank and destroying the judge's flower garden.

The pilot of the ship is supposed to have been the only one on board, and while his remains are badly disfigured, enough of the original has been picked up to show that he was not an inhabitant of this world.

Mr. T. J. Weems, the United States Signal Service officer at this place and an authority on astronomy, gives it as his opinion that he was a native of the planet Mars.

Papers found on his person—evidently the record of his travels—are written in some unknown hieroglyphics, and cannot be deciphered.

The ship was too badly wrecked to form any conclusion as to its construction or motive power. It was built of an unknown metal, resembling somewhat a mixture of aluminum and silver, and it must have weighed several tons.

The town is full of people to-day who are viewing the wreck and gathering specimens of the strange metal from the debris. The pilot's funeral will take place at noon tomorrow.

> *S. E. Haydon,* Fort Worth Record, *1897 (Haydon and Proctor were Aurora businessmen with a sense of humor; Weems was actually the town blacksmith.)*

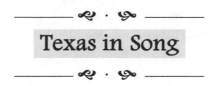

Texas in Song

Will you come to the bower I have shaded for you?
Our bed shall be roses all spangled with dew.
There under the bower of roses you'll lie
With a blush on your cheek, but a smile in your eye.

> *Tune sung by Texans during the charge at San Jacinto, 1836*

Dulces and cigaritos,
Song and the mandolin!
That gory swamp is a gruesome grove
To dance fandangoes in.
We bridged the bog with the sprawling herd
That fell in that frantic rout;
We slew and slew till the sun set red,
And the Texan star flashed out.

> *From John Williamson Palmer's "Fight at the San Jacinto"*

Now I tell what I knew in Texas in my early youth;
(I tell not the fall of Alamo,
Not one escaped to tell the fall of Alamo,
The hundred and fifty are dumb yet at Alamo;)
'Tis the tale of the murder in cold blood of four hundred and
twelve young men.

Retreating, they had form'd in a hollow square, with their bag-
gage for breastworks;
Nine hundred lives out of the surrounding enemy's, nine
times their number, was the price they took in advance;
Their colonel was wounded and their ammunition gone;

They treated for an honorable capitulation, receiv'd writing and seal, gave up their arms, and march'd back prisoners of war.

They were the glory of the race of rangers;
Matchless with horse, rifle, song, supper, courtship,
Large, turbulent, generous, handsome, proud, and affectionate,
Bearded, sunburnt, drest in the free costume of hunters,
Not a single one over thirty years of age.

The second First-day morning they were brought out in squads, and massacred, it was beautiful early summer;
The work commenced about five o clock, and was over by eight.
None obey'd the command to kneel;
Some made a mad and helpless rush, some stood stark and straight;
A few fell at once, shot in the temple or heart, the living and dead lay together;
The maim'd and mangled dug in the dirt, the newcomers saw them there;
Some, half-kill'd, attempted to crawl away;
These were despatch'd with bayonets, or batter'd with the blunts of muskets;
A youth not seventeen years old seiz'd his assassin till two more came to release him;
The three were all torn, and cover'd with the boy's blood.

At eleven o'clock began the burning of the bodies:
That is the tale of the murder of the four hundred and twelve young men.
Walt Whitman, "Song of Myself," Leaves of Grass, 1855

So now I'm marching southward, my heart is full of woe;
I'm going back to Georgia to see my Uncle Joe.
You may talk about your Beauregard and sing of General Lee,
But the gallant Hood of Texas played hell in Tennessee.

> *Altered lyrics of "The Yellow Rose of Texas," after General
> John Bell Hood's disastrous defeat at Nashville, 1864*

She would hunger that I might eat,
Would take the bitter and leave me the sweet;
But once, when I made her jealous for fun
At something I whispered or looked or done,
One Sunday, in San Antonio,
To a glorious girl in the Alamo,
She drew from her garter a little dagger,
And—sting of a wasp—it made me stagger!
An inch to the left, or an inch to the right,
And I shouldn't be maundering here tonight;
But she sobbed, and sobbing, so quickly bound
Her torn rebosa about the wound
That I swiftly forgave her. Scratches don't count
In Texas, down by the Rio Grande.

> *From "Lasca," by Frank Desprez, 1882*

Before the first verse was finished, the house was in an uproar and by the time "til Gabriel blows his horn" was reached the audience was semi-hysterical. They pounded the floor and shouted for an encore which the quartet willingly gave again and again and still again until the students themselves were joining with them and the singers were hoarse.

> Dallas News, *on the premiere of "The Eyes of Texas" at
> Hancock Opera House, Austin, 1904*

When you go down on Deep Ellum,
Put your money in your socks,
'Cause them women on Deep Ellum
'Sho will throw you on the rocks.
Huddie "Leadbelly" Ledbetter, 1917

So Long, It's Been Good to Know You
Woody Guthrie, song title inspired by the onset of the Dust Bowl, 1934

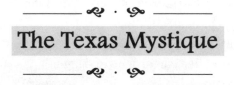

The Texas Mystique

The meeting of the "First Congress of the Republic of Texas" will be in a few days—the course it may pursue involves our future destiny, and the prayers of all should ascend on high that the result may be auspicious. To those who compose that body, I would say, in the language of the Holy Writ, when you enter the sacred hall, "Throw off your shoes for the ground on which you stand is Holy."
"Patrick Henry" writes to the Telegraph and Texas Register, *on the imminent inaugural session of the legislature of the new Republic—in a five-room storehouse of W. C. White & Co., in Columbia, 1836*

Texans ignore "better," long ago forgot the useless word "good." Everything in Texas is "best."
Edward Smith, Account of a Journey Through North-Eastern Texas, *1849*

When we hear a man say "Texan," we involuntarily look to see if he has the lock-jaw, or if he has ice in his mouth. There is not excuse for a man to use such a word in a mild climate. The genius of our language requires generally the termination "ian," when it is necessary to give the name to the inhabitants of that country. "Texian" is the name for which we fought, and which shows ourselves independent of all foreign dictation. Let us stand up for the rights of the "old Texian" against the ruthless Goths and Vandals who are endeavoring to deprive him of that which has blazed so brilliantly from the folds of his banner over all his battle-fields.

From a debate in The Texas Monument, *1851*

In America, the Bostonian looks down upon the Virginian—the Virginian on the Tennesseeian—the Tennesseeian on the Alabamian—the Alabamian on the Mississippian—the Mississippian on the Louisianian—the Louisianian on the Texian—the Texian on New Mexico, and we suppose, New Mexico on Pandemonium.

Joseph Baldwin, The Flush Times of Alabama and Mississippi, *1853*

You may ride in one day from odorous, moss-grown forests, where everything is of tropic fullness, into a section where the mesquite and chaparral dot the gaunt prairie here and there; or from the sea-loving populations of Galveston and her thirty-mile beach, to peoples who have never seen a mast or a wave, and whose main idea of water is that it is something difficult to find and agreeable as a beverage.

Edward King, The Great South, *1875*

The Typical Texan is a large-sized Jabberwock, a hairy kind of gorilla, who is supposed to ride on a horse. He is a half-alligator, half-human, who eats raw buffalo, and sleeps out on the prairie.

Alexander Sweet looks at the distorted perceptions common among people outside the Lone Star State, in Texas Siftings, *1882*

No one ever leaves Texas after they have been here a certain length of time. They either can't or don't want to, or it may be as the old settlers used to say, "having once drunk Red River water, it was not possible to go back"; the fact remains, few people seem to come here with a view of staying, but they do stay and have stayed until nearly three millions are here, and there are "more to follow."

H. H. McConnell, veteran of the 6th U.S. Cavalry, in Five Years a Cavalryman, or Sketches of Regular Army Life on the Texas Frontier, *1889*

Writers facing the problem of Texas find themselves floundering in generalities, and I am no exception. Texas is a state of mind. Texas is an obsession. Above all, Texas is a nation in every sense of the word. And there's an opening covey of generalities.

John Steinbeck, Travels With Charley, *1962*

Most areas in the world may be placed in latitude and longitude, described chemically in their earth, sky and water, rooted and fuzzed over with identified flora and populated with known fauna, and there's an end to it. Then there are others where fable, myth, preconception, love, longing, or prejudice step in and so distort a cool, clear appraisal that a kind of high-colored magical confusion takes permanent hold. Greece is such an area, and those parts of England where King Arthur walked. One quality of such places as

I am trying to define is that a very large part of them is personal and subjective. And surely Texas is such a place.

    John Steinbeck, Travels With Charley, *1962*

There are, in round numbers, about twelve million of us, and I'll cross my heart and hope to burn in hell if you'll see most of us on a horse or in a Cadillac, except maybe once a year at rodeo time or when some show-off invites us to the country club. It is true that we have horses in Texas—more than ever before—but the one in every forty Texans who owns a horse is way behind the one in every ten Texans who has a pickup truck. But watch your generalizations! This does not mean that every pickup has a rifle rack in the rear window and a citizen's band radio on the dash. Just as it does not mean that every Texan who drives a Cadillac is a millionaire. We do carry guns fairly freely, and we do talk by radio on the road of life, and indigestion knows we love bourbon and beer, barbecue and chicken-fried steak, but it would be inaccurate to hold up the redneck beside the cowboy and the millionaire as a symbol of the new Texas. We are too diverse a people; we simply dwarf, in numbers and subtlety, that exaggerated and grotesque trinity.

    Bill Porterfield, Introduction to A Loose Herd of Texans, *1978*

When Alaska achieved statehood Texas did not for a moment surrender its historic place in the grammar of American language and braggadocio: big, bigger, biggest, Texan. Texans argue that while Alaska is twice as large in terms of crude bulk it is Texas that remains, in more significant ways, powerful, grand and pre-eminent, the basic American metaphor for size, grossness, power, wealth, ambition, high-rolling, and boasting: in a word, Texanic.

    Trevor Fishlock, The State of America, *1986*

Once I said to a Texas soldier, "You're beautiful," and he answered me, "Ma'am, you should never say that to a man."

"And what should I say to a man?"

"In Texas," he replied, "the most you can say to a man is that his pants fit him well."

> *Marlene Dietrich,* Marlene, *1989*

My suspicion is that Prince Charles, after his dynamic visitation here in 1986 for our double-jump-up, jim-dandy Sesquicentennial, went home and told the queen: "Jeez, Mom, you have gotta go to Texas. You will not believe that place"...I say we just lay it out there and show her why we're different. Bring on the Kilgore Rangerettes, the Dallas Cowboy Cheerleaders, the Aggie band, a rattlesnake round-up, Speaker Lewis and the entire Legislature, the Cotton-Eyed Joe, a couple of feedlots, three rodeos, four honky-tonks, and a partridge in a pear tree. Remember the state motto: Too Much Is Not Enough, and Wretched Excess Is Even More Fun.

> *Molly Ivins, "Capitalizing on the Queen's Visit to This Here Fine State,"* Nothin' But Good Times Ahead, *1993*

Fencing meant the end of open ranges, the end of the nomadic cowboy, the end of his yondering spirit, his freedom. The West was gone and what followed was *The West*, and in *The West* the cowboy was no longer a serf for those prairie Caesars, the ranchers, but a kind of dauntless Cossack of the plains riding his white stallion across the prairie with the speed of summer lightning, delivering justice to an unjust world. *The West* is the Texas of official legend, a mythical country with its straight-line horizon and flat vacant space, the Texas of hard-bellied, lean-hipped Clint Eastwoods and Gary Coopers with dark, dangerous eyes. This is pulp magazine and paperback book Texas, Saturday matinee Texas, the cine-vérité state of celluloid heroism, six-gun valor, saloon-and-sarsaparilla true grit. Hollywood grew wealthy from *The West* and outsiders believed, perhaps still believe, the boots-and-jeans and shoot-em-up stereotype, still suppose that *The West* lives on in the hearts of free men everywhere. God knows, we Texans have gone to preposterous lengths to preserve those vainglorious legends.

> *Jerry Flemmons,* Amon: the Texan Who Played Cowboy for America, *1998*

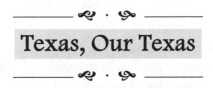

Texas, Our Texas

I'm a dead man, boys, but don't let the others know it; keep on fighting to the death.

> *Richard "Big Dick" Andrews, first fatality in the Texas Revolution, Concepcion, 1835*

Ubi Libertas habitat, ibi nostra patria est [Where Liberty dwells, there is our country]

> *First flag of Texas rebellion, 1835*

I have had a flag made the colours, and their arrangement the same as the old one—with the words and figures, "Constitution of 1824," displayed on the white, in the centre.

> *Philip Dimmitt, writing to Stephen F. Austin from Goliad in 1835, describes the flag which, according to tradition, flew over the Alamo in the final siege*

Mr. Gant—I take the responsibility of taking your overcoat and gun—Your gun they would have had anyhow and I might as well have it as anyone else—If I live to return, I will satisfy you for all—If I die, I leave my clothes to do the best you can with—You can sell them for something. If you overtake me, you can take your rifle and I will trust to chance—The hurry of the moment and my want of means to do better are all the excuse—Forgive the presumption and remember your friend.

Asa Walker

Asa Walker apologizes for appropriating Doctor William W. Gant's rifle, as he rushes to the siege of San Antonio de Béxar and, later, his death at the Alamo, 1835

There it is—come and take it!

Response from Texians of Gonzales to Mexican demands that they surrender their cannon, 1835

I think we are in a hell of a fix. Let's go over to the saloon and get a drink, then mount our horses, go fight like the devil, and get out of it.

Secretary of War T. J. Rusk, Washington-on-the-Brazos, 1836

I am nothing more than an individual citizen of this country, but I feel a more lively interest for its welfare than can be expressed—one that is greatly superior to all pecuniary or personal views of any kind. The prosperity of Texas has been the object of my labors, the idol of my existence. It has assumed the character of a *religion*, for the guidance of my thoughts and actions, for fifteen years.

Stephen F. Austin, 1836

We remain a "Surly little independent Republic" with all our blushing honors thick upon us.

> *Anson Jones, minister to the United States, on the withdrawal of the Texas proposal of annexation, 1838*

[A] blue perpendicular stripe of the width of one-third of the whole length of the flag, with a white star of five points in the center thereof, and two horizontal stripes of equal breadth, the upper stripe white, the lower red, of the length of two-thirds of the whole length of the flag.

> *Specification of the Lone Star flag by the Texas Legislature, 1839*

The enemy are all around me on every side; but I fear them not. I will hold my position until I hear from reinforcements. Come and help me—it is the most favorable opportunity I have ever seen. There are eleven hundred of the enemy. I can whip them on my own ground, without any help, but I cannot take prisoners. Why don't you come?—Huzza! huzza for Texas.

> *Captain Mathew Caldwell, Salado Creek, 1842*

I am sorry, now, that I was not in that battle [San Jacinto], for, if I had been, my Texas record would now be complete. And, really, if I had known how few of you would have been killed, I would most certainly have been there.

> *Former governor Francis Lubbock, speaking to a group of veterans, 1894*

Honor the Texas flag. I pledge allegiance to thee, Texas, one and indivisible.

> *Official salute to the flag of Texas, adopted in 1965*

Texas is my mind's country, that place I most want to understand and record and preserve. Four generations of my people sleep in its soil; I have children there, and a grandson; the dead past and the living future tie me to it. Not that I always approve it or love it. It vexes and outrages and disappoints me—especially when I am there. It is now the third most urbanized state, behind New York and California, with all the tangle, stench, random violence, architectural rape, historical pillage, neon blight, pollution, and ecological imbalance the term implies. Money and mindless growth remain high on the list of official priorities, breeding a crass boosterism not entirely papered over by an infectious energy. The state legislature—though improving as slowly as an old man's mending bones—still harbors excessive, coon-ass, rural Tory Democrats who fail to understand that 79.7 percent of Texans have flocked to urban areas and may need fewer farm-to-market roads, hide-and-tick inspectors, or outraged orations almost comically declaiming against welfare loafers, creeping socialism, the meddling ol' feds, and sin in the aggregate.

> *Larry L. King, "Playing Cowboy,"* Warning: Writer at Work, *1985*

I love the state of Texas, but I regard that as a harmless perversion on my part and would not, in the name of common humanity, try to foist my pathology off on anyone else.

> *Molly Ivins, "Texas Observed,"* Molly Ivins Can't Say That, Can She?, *1991*

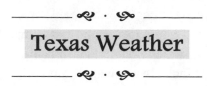

Texas Weather

(see **Blue Northers** and **Storm of the Century**)

Rain! why it falls in torrents. And muddy! whoppee!! If there is a town in Texas more muddy than this pleas tell the Bishop not to send me to it.
> *Pastor C. H. Brooks, Houston, 1856*

We have dust everywhere. Dust in the street, dust in the air, dust in the houses. The streets are filled with dust. We eat dust, breathe dust, walk in dust, sit in dust. Dust rises in clouds on every puff of air, and floats about as though it had no gravity. It settles on everything. If never before, our dusty citizens can now realize the meaning of the words dust thou art, and unto dust thou shalt return.
> Houston Tri-Weekly Telegraph, *1858*

We are destitute. The town is gone. One-tenth of the population are dead. Dead bodies are strewn for twenty miles along the bay. Nine-tenths of the houses are destroyed. Send us help, for God's sake.
> *Message from W. H. Crain to the editor of the* Galveston News, *after a hurricane obliterated Indianola, 1875*

The Amarillo Improvement Company is putting a flagstaff on the Opera House for the use of the weather bureau. The flags will be hoisted each day about noon and will be good for the following day.

A white flag indicates fair weather. A blue flag indicates rain or snow. A white and blue flag indicates local rain, while a white flag with a black square in the center is the cold wave flag and indicates a fall of 15 degrees in temperature and to a temperature below 45 degrees. The black triangle flag, high, indicates higher temperatures and low it indicates lower temperatures. Its absence indicates stationary temperature.

> Amarillo Champion, *1892*

The legislature convenes at Austin, near the centre of the state, and, while the representative from Rio Grande country is gathering his palm leaf fan and his linen duster to set out for the capital, the Pan-handle solon winds his muffler above his well-buttoned overcoat and kicks the snow from his well-greased boots ready for the same journey.

> *O. Henry, "A Departmental Case,"* Ainslee's Magazine, *1902*

To show you how short a time the cyclone lasted, I will tell you everything I thought of from the time I started through the air till I struck the ground; you know how fast you can think. As I whirled out of the door, I thought "Well I have read of this kind of thing—meaning cyclone—but never realized it before." Then I remembered telling a neighbor, when she spoke of our house being strong, "I don't want these rock walls piled in on me. If I knew a cyclone was coming, I would run away from this house as fast as I could." Then the storm was over and I was getting up.

> *Mrs. J. G. Adams of Glen Rose describes being lifted bodily by the 1902 tornado that killed six townspeople*

In these experiments we are following a practice that absolutely and unfailingly did produce rain during the Civil War. Every man who was in battle knows that rain invariably followed the heavy concussions, and an old soldier told me the other day that during a twenty-one day bombardment the rain began after the first day

C. W. Post, who founded a breakfast cereal empire in Battle Creek, Michigan, before he acquired a quarter-million-acre ranch in the Texas Panhandle, where he experimented with social planning and rain-making.

The UT Institute of Texan Cultures at San Antonio No. 79-159 Courtesy of Tex Cook and continued more or less during the total twenty days following. I am spending a considerable amount of money in these experiments, and I want to have you carry them on carefully. I want extra-ordinary attention given to this subject, for it means a very great deal to the country at large and all of us included.

> *Instructions from cereal millionaire C. W. Post on his attempts to stimulate rain with dynamite exploded from kites, 1911*

We camped one night on a pretty grass plot. After night there was a Texas shower, and soon there was six inches of water in our tents; and I made my first military mental note: When you see a green spot in Texas ask why, before you camp there.

> *Colonel Percy M. Ashburn remembers a lesson learned when he was an army doctor new to Texas, in his* History of the Medical Department of the United States Army, *1929*

Barring acts of God or unforeseen personal tragedy, or illness, I pledge myself to be the LAST MAN to leave this country...

> *From the oath of the Last Man Club, organized by John McCarty of the* Dalhart Texan *during the Dust Bowl, 1935*

There is in the Texas climate one constant—wind. It may be a waft or it may be a gale, but it never lets up. Texans seldom use the word "wind" in referring to the ever-present phenomenon. "We always have a nice breeze," they are likely to say, frequently holding on to their hats.

> *John Bainbridge,* The Super-Americans, *1961*

That's Entertainment

The Public are respectfully informed that the Scenery, which was materially injured in the voyage from the United States, having been repaired by Messrs. Chambers & Jackson, the Company will have the honor of making their appearance on Monday Evening, June 11, 1838; When will be presented Sheridan Knowles' celebrated Comedy of The Hunchback. Previous to the Comedy, Mr. Carlos will recite an Opening Address. After which the whole Company will sing A New National Texian Anthem, Written expressly for the occasion by Mr. Corri. The Whole to conclude with the popular farce of The Dumb Belle, or I'm Perfection. The members of the Orchestra having not yet arrived from Mobile, the Managers request the kind indulgence of their patrons for a few days.

> *Handbill of the first performance by a professional stage troupe in Texas, Houston, 1838*

The audience arrived when it was first treated to the tuning of what had once been a piano, but more appropriately now might be called a collection of tin kettles. Well, the piano was screwed up to G#, and after a considerable time passed in tuning—the audience tired of waiting—the concert commenced with a quartette. Before it was concluded, there was a regular breakdown. Our Prima—and only Donna—a delicate young lady, Mrs. Sealsfield found that the instrument was in as base a B flat as one could possibly wish. It was no go...

According to the program it was my turn. A Spanish song was given, at the end of which "Bueno, bueno, muy bonito" from the Spaniards—but from the Texas citizens resounded "Give us a

song from the old country." I gave them one, breathing as much of trumpets, drums, powder and shot, etc. as the most Hector-like could wish for. Encored of course, and amongst other protestations of eternal and everlasting friendship were the following: "Now if that stranger wants a town lot here, I'll give him one." "If he stops in the country and will run for Congress, he has my vote." "They say he's a lawyer; why, we'll make him a judge ere long."
    William Bollaert, diary, 1842

BETROTHED'S NIGHTMARE
A Horrible Adventure
Ascending Mt. Blanch
A Wonderful Flame
Amateur Night
One week's program of silent movies at the Lyric Theatre, Greenville, 1907 (shows at 2:30, 7:30, 8:45 daily)

The first part of the performance went fairly well, but in the middle of the show the audience suddenly got up en masse and disappeared through the front exit. Investigation disclosed that the customers had gone outside to view a runaway mule.

My father and his brother, though accustomed to insults, were enraged by this one. When the customers filed back into the theater, thirty minutes later, the Marx brothers were no longer interested in giving a good performance. All they wanted to do was get even with the audience, and the only way they knew how was to burlesque the kind of singing they had been doing so seriously.

This quickly evolved into a roughhouse comedy bit, with the Marxes, led by my father, flinging insults about Texas and its inhabitants to the audience as rapidly as they could think of them.

My father is not very clear about the exact phraseology of some of these insults, but he does remember calling the Texans in

the audience "damned Yankees" and throwing in a couple of lines
that went something like:

> *Nacogdoches*
> *Is full of roaches.*

And:

> *The Jackass*
> *Is the finest*
> *Flower of*
> *Tex-ass.*

They were not looking for laughs; they fully expected to be
tarred and feathered and run out of town on a rail. But instead the
audience loved their clowning and greeted their insults and most
tired jokes with uproarious laughter.

> *The metamorphosis of a mediocre wandering vaudeville
> troupe called The Four Nightingales into the immortal Marx
> Brothers, triggered by a rude Nacogdoches crowd in 1920, as
> told by Groucho's son Arthur in* My Life With Groucho,
> *1954*

Times are hard, Sonny, and fat ladies eat too much, so we ain't got
one this year. We got four midget shows instead.

> *Sideshow manager's explanation to a boy looking for the fat
> lady at the 1931 State Fair*

Go to Dallas for Education, Come to Fort Worth for Entertainment.

> *Advertisement for Fort Worth's Frontier Centennial Exposition, 1936 (whose enticements included Sally Rand's "Nude
> Ranch")*

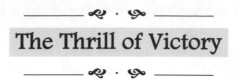

The Thrill of Victory

I am not decrying football—I incline to the view that an occasional rough-and-tumble scrapping match in which there is imminent danger of black eyes, and even of broken bones, is good for a boy. I simply point out that as an intellectual game it not only ranks below chess, billiards, and baseball, but does not even rise to a parity with pugilism.

> *William Cowper Brann,* The Iconoclast

I've seen them wear six-shooters to games in the Texas League, and when a fan pulled one out in Fort Worth and took a shot at a fly ball, I was ready to check out.

> *Former umpire "Wild Bill" Setley recalls the turbulent 1910 season*

Find a way to keep people in their seats at halftime.

> *B. E. Masters, president of Kilgore College, to Gussie Nell Davis, who responded by forming the Kilgore Rangerettes, 1939*

We got all the breaks and they were all bad.

> *Coach Jimmy Phelan, after the Dallas Texans NFL franchise ended its first and last season with only one victory, 1952*

But why, some say, the moon? Why choose this as our goal? And they may well ask why climb the highest mountain? Why, 35 years ago, fly the Atlantic? Why does Rice play Texas?

President John F. Kennedy, speaking at Rice University about the goal of putting an American on the moon, 1962

Sectional football games have the glory and the despair of war, and when a Texas team takes the field against a foreign state, it is an army with banners.

John Steinbeck, Travels with Charley, *1962*

America's Team

First applied to the Dallas Cowboys by Bob Ryan, 1978

The rest of the world is sweeping past us. The oil and gas of the Texas future is the well-educated mind. But we are still worried about whether Midland can beat Odessa at football.

Governor Mark White, advocating a "no pass, no play" policy in Texas public schools, 1985

What difference does the uniform make? You don't hit with it.

Yogi Berra, new coach of the Houston Astros, 1986

The Town Booster

But let it not be supposed that we in Houston are going to sit down like children, and cry because we have dropped our bread and butter, although it *has* fallen on the "buttered side." Not we, nothing can be farther from our thoughts than this. We *will* have a great city, in spite of them, and if they dont behave very well up there in Austin, we will *cut off their supplies*, and throw them upon corn bread and beef.

> *Houston* Morning Star, *on the relocation of the capital from Houston to Austin, 1839*

[Houston] is the ambitious rival of Galveston, and because nature has endowed its streets with unusual capacity for muddiness, Galveston calls its inhabitants "mud-turtles." A free exchange of satiric compliments between the two infant cities is of frequent occurrence.

> *Edward King,* The Great South, *1875*

Of seven newspapers in the Panhandle each claims its town to be the present and prospective metropolis. As a matter of fact, there are and will be some good towns in the Panhandle, but the rest need only settle among themselves the question of second place, for Tascosa will inevitably rank first. Evidences of the fact accumulate every day.

> Tascosa Pioneer, *1887*

Hemphill County, CANADIAN, the County Seat. The Eldorado of the West. The Greatest Cattle Shipping Point in the World. Bound to eclipse All Other Cities within 250 miles of Her. The Best City Platted in 25 years. Backed by Millions.

Canadian Free Press, *1887*

Now that railroads are penetrating the country, a new industry will spring up and assume surprising dimensions, and there are millions in it, Bones! Reports have it that in various parts of the Panhandle, tons and tons of these are being gathered for early sale.

> *The millions of buffalo skeletons scattered across the prairie by hunters were a valuable source of minerals, as pointed out in the* Tascosa Pioneer, *1887*

Do you want a rich black sandy loam? We have it. Do you want a rich chocolate soil? It is here. Do you want highly fertile red soil? We have plenty of it here. Do you want black prairie land? There is plenty of it here. Do you want river bottom, valley land, table land, smooth level prairie, heavily timbered or open prairie land? You can find all of these in Jones County. We have the finest lands that can be found in Texas.

West Texas is the best part of the State, and Jones County is the garden spot of the West...

There are but two or three negroes in Jones County, and we don't want any more. We find that we can get along better without them. This is a white man's country, and it is not degrading for a white man to work. Keep the negro out and learn your children how to work. That is the idea.

You can grow anything in Jones County except negroes and tropical fruits...

Not a saloon in Jones County. Do you know that we consider this the grandest thing that could be said in our favor? Not a saloon in Jones County! Does not that one sentence speak volumes in favor of the morality and sobriety of our town and country?

From Jones County, Texas: A Monthly Publication for Home-Seekers, *1891*

Amarillo is literally full of hogs, and the flea crop is very promising—getting ready for the summer visitors. Get another press convention and protracted meeting and invalids coming in needn't bring any flesh brush or other skin irritants. Amarillo will throw in the fleas with the board and lodging. Come along.
Amarillo News, *1895*

Another special feature of Sour Lake, that alone is sufficient to make it famous, is the springs that cure women of those diseases that are particular to their sex and nine out of ten women are thus afflicted. Another feature peculiar to Sour Lake is the tars that bubble up through the mineral springs and float on the water like cream. It contains more mineral salts and has proven to be the best ointment known for all kinds of sores, ulcers, skarslous or syphilitic boils, carbuncles, burns, bruises, rheumatism, piles and other skin eruptions—as well as for sore throat, ulcers and catarrh of the stomach, diphtheria, etc. When atomized and inhaled, it is very beneficial in the case of pneumonia, consumption, bronchitis and all colds in the bronchial tubes and lungs. It has been used very successfully for twenty years in the infirmary of Houston by Dr. Stewart and Dr. Boile. Besides these special features, which no other health resort has, it is well known that Sour Lake sulphur, iron, soda and acid water and baths will speedily cure diphtheria, indigestion and all kinds of stomach and liver and kidney complaints. Chronic diarrhea, chronic malaria, rheumatism, paralysis, nervous disorders, chronic inebriety or blood poison and it is also a blood purifier.
Prospectus of the Sour Lake Company, 1896

You might mention that N. Cohn observed the Jewish New Year
5660 Monday. This will let the new people who are settling here
know that Alice has a Jew store and that's a good thing for the
town for it is a drawing card.

Alice Echo, *1899*

A very interesting session was held last Saturday morning in the
offices of the First National Bank when one of the knockers was
invited to give an account of himself. Business men had known for
some time that this man had been doing underhanded work, mis-
representing the business men and community to strangers,
sending out destructive letters to prospective settlers here, and
endeavoring to either make real estate deals himself or fix it so the
other men could not close a deal. A crowd of business men gathered and the culprit was placed on the witness stand. At first he
denied charges but when facts and proofs were presented he
mildly admitted that he had sent out certain letters and talked with
certain men, but certainly didn't mean any harm at all. A few more
scrimmages, denials, and proofs, and the man sailed out of the
room after telling the crowd what he thought of them.

Randall County News, *1910*

Friend:

We have used in our family Post's cereals and Postum for years,
but never until within the last few hours did we hear of Post's City
of Homesteads. Do write me *all* about the scheme. Do you have
literature regarding the same?

In haste,

Yours for success,
Mrs. A. B. Schultz

P.S.   Is the soil sandy?
        Does the wind blow?

Do you have flees?
Does it snow in winter?
A letter to inquire about C. W. Post's planned community in the Panhandle, 1911

That man wants the whole government of the United States to be run for the exclusive benefit of Fort Worth, and if possible, for the detriment of Dallas.

> *Vice President John Nance Garner, on Amon Carter: newspaperman, philanthropist, and Fort Worth's staunchest defender against its evil twin city, Dallas*

A Truly Criminal Justice System

Hear ye, hear ye, court for the Third District is either now in session or by God somebody's going to get killed.

> *Judge Robert McAlpin "Three-Legged Willie" Williamson, 1838*

[Lynch] law has been as generally villified as it has been generally successful. It is seldom that the judgment of the respectable part of a community errs, or that a punishment inflicted by it is disproportional to the crime, & at all events this much can be said of Lynch law, that it has reached murderers, felons, & swindlers *when no other law could*, who would in all probability be even now prowling about the country in the exercise of their several avocations.

> *Francis C. Sheridan,* Galveston Island, *1840*

The Court was over a crockery store used on Sunday for a Methodist Chapel—the Judge, chewing his quid, thrown back in his chair, his legs thrown up on his desk—the District Attorney, chewing and smoking—the Council for the prisoner, D°. D°. and a small quantity of whittling—indeed I saw the weed in the mouths of some of the lookers on. Order was kept in the court, but ever and anon a squirt of tobacco juice on the floor.

    William Bollaert, diary, 1842

It is doubtful whether in the whole history of trial by jury a more remarkable scene than the one here presented was ever exhibited. The trial took place in one of the adobe or mud-built houses peculiar to the country, which was dimly lighted from a single small window. Scarcely an individual was present who had not the appearance and garb of men who spend their lives on the frontier, far from civilization and its softening influences.... There sat the judge, with a pistol lying on the table before him; the clerks and attorneys wore revolvers at their sides; and the jurors were either armed with similar weapons, or carried with them the unerring rifle....The fair but sunburnt complexion of the American portion of the jury, with their weapons resting against their shoulders, and pipes in their mouths, presented a striking contrast to the swarthy features of the Mexicans, muffled in checkered *serapes*, holding their broad-brimmed glazed hats in their hands, and delicate cigarritos in their lips. The reckless unconcerned appearance of the prisoners, whose unshaven faces and dishevelled hair gave them the appearance of Italian bandits rather than of Americans or Englishmen; the grave and determined bearing of the bench; the varied costume and expression of the spectators and members of the Commission, clad in serapes, blankets, or overcoats, with their different weapons, and generally with long beards, made altogether one of the most remarkable groups which ever graced a courtroom.

> *Boundary Commissioner John Russell Bartlett describes the picturesque trial of three American toughs for the murder of a Commission employee, for which they were soon hanged, El Paso, 1851*

It is only a Mexican, a simpleton or a coward that would appeal to law for justice.

> *Emmanuel Henri Dieudonné Domenech,* Missionary Adventures in Texas and Mexico, *1852*

"Killed in attempting to escape." "Killed while resisting arrest." These are two expressions that are fast coming to have a melancholy and terrible significance to the people of Western Texas. They furnish the brief epitaph to the scores who have fallen and are falling victims to the ignorance, the arrogance, or the brutality of those charged with the execution of the law.

> *Editorial in the* Victoria Advocate *in protest of abuses by the State Police, 1870*

Last night about thirty men rode up to the Mat Wallace's house about three-fourths of a mile from the public square, called him out, took him about fifty yards and hung him to a tree. The tree being low they tied a rope to his feet and tied it to another tree to prevent him from touching the ground.

> *The* Galveston News *reports a peculiar lynching in Waco, 1875*

I can straddle every goddamned alderman here.

> *Marshal Dallas Stoudenmire to the El Paso city council, as it considered a motion to remove him from office, 1882*

An expression of the will of the people.

> *County Attorney O. P. Moore's view of the lynching of teenag-*
> *ers Ben Mitchell and Ernest Collins in Columbus after they*
> *confessed to the murder of a nineteen-year-old girl, 1935*

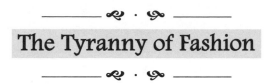

The Tyranny of Fashion

I am well enough, for my neighbor is no better; and what does it signify in this new country how I dress? A leather hunting shirt, and a pair of buckskin breeches, are good enough for the mud and briers; besides I believe I'll just go and hunt a little to day, which will make me dirty enough before I return.

> *David B. Edward describes, with some distaste, the attitude*
> *common among his fellow pioneers of the De Witt Colony, in*
> The History of Texas; or the Emigrant's, Farmer's and
> Politician's Guide to the Character, Climate, Soil, and Pro-
> duction of That Country: Geographically Arranged from
> Personal Observations and Experience, *1836*

Don't take any country dresses for Hanka, because she will not need them here. Our country dresses are the reason that the native people make fun of us and they cause sin.

> *Father Leopold Moczygemba, founder of the Polish settle-*
> *ment at Panna Maria, writes home to Silesia about the*
> *scandal created by the traditional dresses of his homeland,*
> *which left as much as* two inches *of ankle visible, 1855*

I saw a powerful fine-looking woman bowing to me, and I bowed, and she bowed, and I bowed again. I didn't know who she was, but

thought maybe she desired to see me, so I started towards her. When I moved, she moved off, with her back to me. Now do you know what was the matter? I was standing on the trail of her dress, and I'll swear I weren't in fifteen feet of her.
    U.S. Senator and former governor Richard Coke

If long hair, part of a sombrero, Mexican spurs, &c., would make a fellow famous, I already occupy a topmost niche in the Temple Frame. If my wild, untamed aspect had not been counteracted by my well-known benevolent and amiable expression of countenance, I would have been arrested long ago by the Rangers on general suspicions of murder and horse stealing. In fact, I owe all my present means of lugubrious living to my desperate and bloodthirsty appearance, combined with the confident and easy way in which I tackle a Winchester rifle.
    William Sydney Porter (O. Henry), letter, 1884

The large lace shoulder cape like those seen in the portraits of the hapless Queen Henrietta Maria are steadily growing in favor. They completely metamorphose a plain costume.

    In skirts, the plain perfect art tailor effects are worn for most occasions. French and English modists agree on this, though the former allow draperies in dressy gowns.

    Brown felt planteaux upon which are parallel rows of black silk braid, are among the novelties shown in new millinery. Hats are bent into becoming shapes, and trimmed with three to five blackbirds. They are stylish.

    The array of basques for skirts, ranging from extreme to the most conservative fullness, are so numerous that anyone can easily find styles to suit her expressed need.

    The latest pocketbooks are of green alligator. Though odd looking affairs, they are said to be the rage. Small suede purses

William Sydney Porter, who years later achieved fame as short story writer O. Henry, poses (front left) with the Hill City Quartette, Austin, 1886.

Texas State Library and Archives Commission

with silver clips are much used. Many are adorned with silver monograms and lined with bright kid.

Silk petticoats for street wear are trimmed with open work embroidery ruffles of silk, like the skirt, over another ruffle of thinner silk, in a bright color, which is considered a vast improvement over laces.

On evening skirts where lace is used, it is pulled over silk flounces, and headed by a twist of ribbon, with bows at intervals all around the skirt.

> Weekly Amarillo News, *1895*

The woman who will sacrifice a songster on the altar of her vanity is wholly devoid of sentiment. There's no more music in her soul than in a ham sandwich, less poetry in her life than can be found in a horned frog. A bird on the bonnet means that the woman beneath it would embalm her baby and wear it as a brooch if Dame Fashion decreed it. A wise husband would hesitate to insure his life in favor of such a woman, for she'd pour hot lead in his ear or dope his dinner to secure the price of a new dress.

> *William Cowper Brann,* The Iconoclast

Parisiana and LaReine Corsets are sold here—Women who wear corsets are the well dressed women. The corset is the dominating feature in a woman's dress, in her whole appearance. If the corset is not correct, the gown cannot be. The corsets sold here are designed to meet the requirements of the latest fashions, made of good material and a large variety of models, so that there is a model for every individual figure. Price 50¢ to $1.00.

> Trinity County Star, *1911*

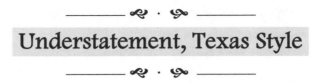

Understatement, Texas Style

A Black Fiend Attacks an Invalid White Lady in Her Bed, Chokes Her Until the Blood Oozes from Her Mouth and Nose, Accomplishes His Design!!
Headline, Fort Worth Daily Democrat, *1879*

A Galveston traveling man writes me as follows:

"I have been for two years past gathering up scraps of your history, and now have the honor to advise you that according to the testimony of many very pious people, among whom are not a few preachers, you are an avowed anarchist who was suspected of being concerned in the Haymarket massacre; that you served two terms in the penitentiary before you were born; that you are a renegade Jew and an Italian Jesuit, that for 30 years you were a Baptist preacher, but were bounced out of the ministry for drunkenness and immorality; that you have been a blasphemous Atheist from your youth up; that you deserted from the federal army in the same year that you were four years old; that you have been discharged from all the Texas dailies for incompetency, and are the author of editorials in the Chicago Inter-Ocean slandering the South; that you are a big over-grown bully who abuses weaker people, and a miserable little poltroon who has been kicked by every cripple between New York and Denver. All this is doubtless correct as far as it goes; now will you please inform me whether you have been guilty of anything else?"

This is a fairly correct list of my crimes thus far; but being still a young man, I may reasonably hope to add to it considerably if not shut off by the sheriff. The greatest drawback to my career as a

criminal is my inability to lie so consistently as some of my dear
brethren in Christ.

> *William Cowper Brann,* The Iconoclast

He could eat centipedes for breakfast and barbed wire for supper
without injuring his digestion; and ride all day and dance all night
without missing a step.

> *Olive Dixon,* The Life of "Billy" Dixon, *1927*

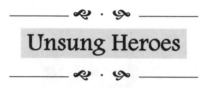

Unsung Heroes

Those legislators who have fought the huge economic special
interests, the racism, and know-nothingism of Texas are pos-
sessed of a special kind of courage. It is not the courage of flashy
deeds done against drear and deadly enemies, but a courage that
often consists of just hanging in there, the courage of those who
outstay boredom, pettiness, mean-mindedness, and stupidity.
They stick through the subcommittee meetings and the committee meetings and the first readings and the second readings and
the conference committee meetings to the final, inevitable screw-
ing. Their courage holds up through the countless failures and
frustrations, and enables them to laugh and get drunk and laugh
some more, and then to try again next session. And there is a
Texas legislative tradition that allows them to respect publicly,
and yes, even love, those canny country bastards who always beat
them.

> *Molly Ivins, "Inside the Texas Fun House,"* Molly Ivins
> Can't Say That, Can She?, *1991*

Wanderlust

Daniel Boone, a native of Carolina, a citizen of Opelousas for twelve years, and, at present, in this post, makes known to you, with the greatest respect, that I have come to this place with my family and goods because those lands have passed into the hands of the Anglo-Americans and it does not suit me to live under their laws. I came to seek your protection in order that if you consider it well, you may order set apart for me a town lot and lands for farming—since this is my occupation.

Atascosito, June 11, 1806

Danl. Boone.

The nephew of the Daniel Boone applies to Spanish authorities for permission to settle at Orcoquisac, no longer pleased to live in Louisiana since it has passed from France to the United States

The landlord was a dry, tough, hard-faced old fellow (not so very old either, for he was but just turned sixty, I should think), who had been out with the militia in the last war with England, and had seen all kinds of service,—except a battle; and he had been very near seeing that, he added: very near. He had all his life been restless and locomotive, with an irresistible desire for change; and was still the son of his old self: for if he had nothing to keep him at home, he said (slightly jerking his hat and his thumb towards the window of the room in which the old lady sat, as we stood talking in front of the house), he would clean up his musket, and be off to Texas to-morrow morning. He was one of the very many descendants of Cain proper to this continent, who seem destined from their birth to serve as pioneers in the great human army: who gladly go on from year to year extending its outposts, and leaving home after home behind them; and die at last, utterly regardless of their graves being left thousands of miles behind, by the wandering generation who succeed.

> *At an inn near Saint Louis, Charles Dickens meets a would-be Gone-to-Texan,* American Notes for General Circulation, *1842*

During breakfast our host informed us that he had in mind to abandon his farm and to move farther up the river. When my companion, who on a previous trip found this man well satisfied with his present home, asked in astonishment what induced him to make such a resolve, he answered in a tone of voice which sounded as though he were suffering from an intolerable condition: "The country is getting too crowded, I cannot live here any longer." This reason seemed peculiar to me since I had seen no houses far and near and I therefore asked him how close the nearest neighbors lived. "Well the next fellow lives but ten miles from here," he answered. I expressed my deep regrets to the man for being so hemmed in and at the same time thought to myself, that it was indeed fortunate that everyone in old Europe did not require so much of the earth's surface as did this old backwoodsman.

> *Doctor Ferdinand Roemer, a visitor from Germany, encounters the urge to keep moving, on the Little River in Williamson County, 1846*

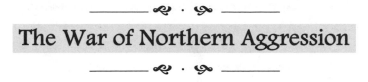

The War of Northern Aggression

A work written by a talented American lady, entitled "Uncle Tom's Cabin," is creating much excitement both sides of the Atlantic... Her design was evidently to pander to the diseased abolition feeling that pervaded some portions of the North a year or so ago.

    San Antonio Ledger, *1853*

I can wipe up with a cambric handkerchief every drop of blood that will be shed in this war.

    State Senator and future governor Fletcher Stockdale, 1861

The boasted valor of Texans has been fully vindicated; Valverde, Glorieta, Albuquerque, Peralta, and last, though not least, your successful and almost unprecedented evacuation, through mountain passes and over a trackless waste of a hundred miles through a famishing country, will be duly chronicled, and form one of the brightest pages in the history of the Second American Revolution.

    Brigadier General Henry H. Sibley's message to his troops makes the Confederate invasion of New Mexico, which ended in a humiliating retreat, sound like a spectacular triumph, 1862

The creeks in this vicinity are said to be full of dead men. I witnessed a sight yesterday which I never wish to see again in a civilized and enlightened country. In a water hole in Spring Creek (about two miles from camp) there are four human bodies lying on top of the water, thrown in and left to rot, and that too after they were hanged by the neck and dead.

> *Sergeant Thomas C. Smith, after the bloody suppression of German immigrants who sympathized with the Union, 1862*

Toward the man who, believing in the justice of his cause, had the courage to shoulder his gun and face his opponents on the field of battle, I harbor no resentment now, but for the cowards who, taking good care to keep out of harm's way, hunted down and murdered defenseless Union men—well, I have never been a believer in the orthodox hell, still, when I think of those wretches, I am forced to concede that it was an oversight in the plan of creation if hell was left out.

> *Noah Smithwick, whose nephew John Hubbard stayed in Texas instead of fleeing to California with his uncle and was killed by secessionist bushwhackers*

Do the generals expect us to be killed and want us to wear our burial shrouds?

> *Troops of 2nd Texas at Shiloh, on being issued undyed, white uniforms, 1862*

They are lying on the field, where you sent them, sir. My division has been almost wiped out!

> *General John Bell Hood to Robert E. Lee at Antietam, after his Texas Brigade stopped a crucial Federal assault, but at a cost of 560 casualties among 854 men, 1862*

Fighting was going on nearly everyday in sight of us; sometimes the Yankee gun boats would get into the Bay among the rebel boats, and at other times they would fight across the narrow strip of land, shooting right over the houses at one another. Many of the cannon balls dropped on the prairie; one of them at one time struck within a few feet of Mr. Williams, almost burying him in the sand as it plowed along on the ground. Poor fellow, he was afterwards killed by one, he carried one home and taking all the powder out of it, as he supposed, set it out in the yard with the hole up, and then told Billy to get him a coal of fire in the tongs. He thought it would just flash a little.

I was present, and not liking the looks of it, crept out behind the picket gates, a few yards away, and peeped between the pickets.

The whole family was looking on to see the fun, Mattie, one of the little girls, was sitting with her arms around a dog's neck, within a few feet of it.

Billy, arriving with the coal, handed it to his father who reached over and let it drop down into the hole—where he had taken out the lead screw.

It seemed to me that the coal hadn't reached the hole when the thing exploded. For a few seconds everything was enveloped in smoke; when the smoke disappeared sufficiently for me to see, the whole sky seemed to be a blaze of fire, and finally Mr. Williams emerged out of the heavy cloud of smoke hopping on one leg.

A piece of the bomb-shell had taken off part of one foot on the left leg and another piece had plowed through the calf of his right leg; part of one ear was also gone. He only lived a few days.

> *Six-year-old Charles A. Siringo on the Matagorda Peninsula in 1862, from* A Texas Cowboy, *1885*

In spite of their peculiar habits of hanging, shooting, &c., which seemed to be natural to people living in a wild and thinly populated country, there was much to like in my fellow travelers.

> *British Colonel Arthur Fremantle, on soldiers of a Texas unit, 1863*

Well he is nothing but a man—about five feet ten inches high—spare made—weighs about 150—has fair hair, blue eyes—red complexion. No mark of greatness about him that may not be found [in] many another Man of no worth at all.

> *Elijah S. C. Robertson's impression of William C. Quantrill, who had just been assigned to round up Confederate deserters in Texas, but soon turned to brigandage against civilians, 1863*

At the outbreak of the war it was found very difficult to raise infantry in Texas, as no Texan walks a yard if he can help it. Many mounted regiments were therefore organized, and afterwards dismounted.

> *British Colonel Arthur Fremantle, an observer during the Civil War, 1863*

I never ordered the Brigade to hold a place, that they did not hold it.

> *General Robert E. Lee, on Hood's Texas Brigade*

Came by Banquete and drew pay for a beef which the quartermaster there had on his books, it having been killed for the troops. The beef was worth $15, but I was paid $2 and that is the first pay I have had for several they killed. Before we were in any danger we had to feed the soldiers with our beeves. As soon as danger threatened we were abandoned and now we are once more out of danger by the withdrawal of the [Union] army, the troops are being sent back to live again on our beeves and the tax collector was the first to remind us the danger was past by his demanding the war tax on property that but a few months ago we had been ordered to abandon to the enemy.

> *Thomas J. Noakes of Corpus Christi grumbles in his diary about the perversities of having to supply Confederate soldiers with meat, 1864*

Some who entered it young came out with broken health and shortened lives; some who entered it in middle age came out with gray hair, impaired memory, and the decrepitude of premature old age. It was a year that had taken much from us and given to us little in return.

> *Colonel Charles C. Nott of the Union army, released in 1865 after thirteen months in Camp Ford, a Confederate prison*

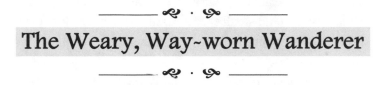

The Weary, Way-worn Wanderer

When bed time came we were ushered into a room where there were several beds. We did not like this much, as we expected a room to ourselves, but on being told that the gentlemen slept on one side and the ladies on the other side of the room, I opened both my eyes and ears and looked again at my hostess, who did not seem to be jesting. Presently several more ladies came in to go to bed. They went through the undressing operation quickly and were all in bed long before we had got over our surprise at this new fashion of sleeping. We soon undressed but did not divest ourselves of all our garments, keeping on outside garments which were calico wrappers. We had only been in bed about an hour when the gentlemen came in one by one until all had retired. I watched with breathless suspense the coming of the last one. This was something we were not accustomed to, and it was several nights before I could sleep—not until nature was completely exhausted and overcome with watching.

Ann Coleman, at a Brazoria inn, 1832, from her journal

The wife of our host, I found, was an intelligent lady from New-York; and her care furnished us with excellent food considering the disadvantages of the place, while her arrangements afforded us more comfort and convenience than we could have expected, in a habitation so disproportioned to our numbers. Our table was set on the ground, in the open passage of the house; while our mattresses were spread at night on the floor of the southern apartment. In order to place thirty men in a horizontal position, on a space about twenty feet square, and each upon a separate bed, required no small care and calculation; yet there we laid ourselves down, as on the floor of a steamboat, and slept soundly till morning.

Anonymous, A Visit to Texas: Being the Journal of a Traveler, *1834*

You are welcomed by a figure in a blue flannel shirt and pendant beard, quoting Tacitus, having in one hand a long pipe, in the other a butcher's knife. Madonnas upon log walls; coffee in tin cups upon Dresden saucers; barrels for seats, to hear a Beethoven's symphony on the grand piano.

Frederick Law Olmsted, A Journey Through Texas, *1857*

We were shown, at the hotel to which we had been recommended, into an exceedingly dirty room, in which two of us slept with another gentleman, who informed us that it was the best room in the house. The outside door, opening upon the ground, had no latch, and during the night it was blown open by the norther, and after we had made two ineffectual attempts to barricade it, was kept open til morning...When the breakfast-bell rung, we all turned out in haste, though our boots were gone and there was no water...

We naturally began to talk of changing our quarters and trying another of the hotels. Then up spoke a dark, sad man at our side—"You can't do better than stay here; I have tried both the others, and I came here yesterday because the one I was at was *too dirty!*" And the man said this, with that leopard-skin pattern of a tablecloth, before him, with those grimy tools in his hands, and with the hostler in his frock, smelling strongly of the stable, just handing him the (No. 3). Never did we see any wholesome food on that table. It was a succession of burnt flesh of swine and bulls, decaying vegetables, and sour and mouldy farinaceous glues, all pervaded with rancid butter.

Frederick Law Olmsted, A Journey Through Texas, *1857*

Whether from the inefficiency of Mr. Nichols' driving, or because Mr. Mather's furious riding frightened the mules, or because the mules were wild, or that the boys had been having a jolly good time on the occasion of the arrival of the first stage, or by a special dispensation of Providence—or from a combination of all these causes—I will not pretend to say, but certainly from some unforeseen and vexatious cause we here suffered a detention of some hours. The mules reared, pitched, twisted, whirled, wheeled, ran, stood still, and cut up all sorts of capers. The wagon performed so many evolutions that I, in fear of my life, abandoned it and took to my heels, fully confident that I could make more progress in a straight line, with much less risk of breaking my neck.

The gyrations continued to considerable length, winding up with tangling all the mules pretty well in the harness, the escape of one of the leaders into the woods, and the complete demolition of the top of the wagon; while those in charge of it lay around loose on the grass, and all were pretty tired and disgusted except those who had nothing to do but look on.

> New York Herald *reporter Waterman Ormsby, the only pas-senger on the inaugural east-west run of the Butterfield Overland Mail, describes a "routine" change of teams at Fort Chadbourne, 1858*

In the long, creaking supper-room, a dirty cloth was laid on a dirtier table, and pork, fried to a cinder and swimming in grease hot enough to scorch the palate, was placed before the guests. To this was presently added, by the hands of a tall, angular, red-haired woman, a yellow mass of dough supposed to be biscuit, a cup of black, bitter bean-juice named coffee, and as a crowning torture, a mustard pot, with very watery mustard in it.

> *Edward King,* The Great South, *1875*

Tascosa's about a hundred miles due northwest, and you can't miss it. Just follow the plain trail of empty whiskey bottles.

> *A rancher's directions to attorney Temple Houston, son of Sam Houston, on the road from Brazoria, 1882*

Mr. Pitt inquired again how far it was to Col. Rivers' place. "Why," said she, "he's our nighest neighbor. We kin e'en a'most hear the chickens crowing over there of a right still mornin—its only five short miles." "Will you be kind enough, madam," said Mr. Pitt, "to give us the direction how to find the way there?" "To be sure," said she. "Do you see that lone tree out yander in the perara [prairie]?" Mr. Pitt said he did. "Well," said she, "keep right straight on to that tree, and arter you pass it 'bout fifty or maybe so a hundred yards, you will come to a cow trail, but don't you take that; go right straight across it, and purty soon you'll come to another; follow that till you get to where it splits, then take the right hand, or ruther, I should say, the left hand split, and it'll carry you into the road to Thompson's Mill. Mind though, you take the left hand split." "I thought it was the right?" said Mr. Pitt. "Did I say the right hand? Well I meant the left hand, anyhow," said she, "and when you get to the mill road follow that till it splits—but you keep the straight forward split to whar it strikes the bottom, and there it sprangles off, so I can't say adzackly which split you do take. Howsomever, 'tain't fur, anyway, from there to Col. Rivers', and I reckon you won't go wrong."

John C. Duval, The Young Explorers, *1892*

Temple Lea Houston: state senator, district attorney, and crack shot.

The UT Institute of Texan Cultures at San Antonio No. 72-3453

What Is in a Name?

Jim! Do you *realize* what you have done to that girl?

> *District Attorney and future governor James Stephen Hogg hears his father-in-law's sorry opinion of the name with which he has just saddled his new daughter, Ima, 1882. ("Ima" was the name of the heroine of a Civil War poem by Jim Hogg's brother Tom.)*

Miss Ima Hogg, art collector and philanthropist, at a shindig in Fredericksburg in 1970.

Texas State Library and Archives Commission

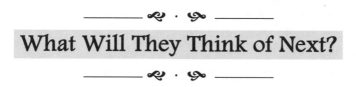

What Will They Think of Next?

Last night there were fifty electric lights burning in the city, and a beautiful light they made. The streets at night are crowded with strangers and citizens going from place to place admiring the wonderful electric light and holiday goods displayed in the various stores.

> *The* Houston Post *pays tribute to Edison's miraculous new invention, December 1882*

E. D. Chambers purchased for his place of business one of the most ingenious pieces of mechanism we have ever seen in the way of a cash register. It is called the "national cash register." It not only registers the amount of your purchase, but also furnishes a ticket showing the name of the article and by whom sold. It is a complete set of books in itself. The only objectional feature it has that keeps every business man from having one is that it costs $300.

Quanah Tribune, *1896*

The almost overwhelming interest of the house was the fact that it had a bathroom on each floor containing a flush commode! When callers came Mother was pleased and happy to show them the conservatory and the new ideas that she had used in many places but they were sometimes reluctant to leave until they had seen the "mechanical commodes." Other houses had had these conveniences for ten years, or longer, but evidently these homes had never been open, as ours was, to the curious *hoi polloi*. So it was that many people had never seen them. For those interested I usually conducted this part of the tour. I remember how they would look up at the water box and lever near the ceiling and how their eyes would then follow the long chain down to its wooden, bulb-shaped end.

"Would you like to see how it works.," I would ask, and immediately they would step back to a safe distance and say, "Yes," in suppressed excitement. After I had gently pulled on the chain, the water would gush down all sides of the bowl and exit with a sucking sound. This was a time when people were becoming aware of the feasibility of this contraption and they were keen to see one in action.

Promptly the town went mad over mechanical commodes. Even the information that a cesspool was necessary, did not dampen their enthusiasm to a marked degree, and little box-like rooms were added to old houses. Some unprogressives didn't approve of their "being right in the house," and with distrust of all "fads" added them off of the back porch, where they could be detached easily when the passing notion had spent itself.

> *Ellen Bowie Holland on the state-of-the-art plumbing in her parents' grand new house in Weatherford in 1900, from* Gay as A Grig, *1963*

Before the days of screens, we all slept under mosquito bars every night. They had a lightweight wood frame that pulled up to the ceiling in the daytime. And by a rope through pulleys, you just pulled it out and let it down. My grandfather would come home for lunch and sit down in the library and they would let the mosquito bar down. He'd take his nap and then go back to the bank.

> *Bill Kirkland recalls Houston at the turn of the century*

Another evidence of the Ozona way of doing things is the installing of an up-to-date covered-in ice wagon, put into service Monday morning by the Ozona Improvement Company, and the horse is wearing harness made by our own harness and saddle maker, Mr.

Arthur Williams. The outfit cost the company considerable money, but in the long run it is money well spent, as ice can be delivered in any kind of weather without lossage.

Ozona Kicker, *1906*

The first local party of automobilists to successfully make a trip from Houston to Galveston and return in a single day made the run on Sunday, leaving here at 6 o'clock in the morning, returning about 9 o'clock in the evening.

Houston Chronicle, *1909*

The human race has gone mad. This will produce more strain than the anatomy can stand. In a few generations, men will be old at 30 and physical wrecks at 40.

A Dallas physician's reaction after Robert Burman drove his Buick 100 miles in 101 minutes, 25 seconds on a dirt track at the State Fair, 1909

LET US WIRE YOUR HOUSE

The long winter nights are coming, You need a good light for reading—Electric light is the only sanitary light—cost less than to keep Kerosene lamps in repair.

PHONE 88

Ad for the Alpine Light and Ice Company, in the Alpine Avalanche, *1916*

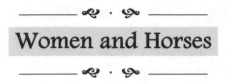

Women and Horses

I had never ridden horseback at Columbus, but my sweetheart wrote me that he had a fine saddle horse for me. Before leaving that place, I had made an up-to-date riding habit which extended below the feet from half a yard to a yard. In 1875 no part of a woman's leg was visible. Looking back I recall a vivid picture of myself on my first horseback ride. Perched upon a sidesaddle, with a habit reaching almost to the ground, I set out. We rode along a trail through a thick wood. What do you suppose happened to my riding habit passing through that brush? It was so badly torn that I had to cut off so much of it that what remained barely covered my feet. It was much more convenient, but it required great care not to expose an ankle, which would have been scandalous.

> *Luvenia Conway Roberts, a ranger's bride in 1875, learns to dress for the frontier, in* A Woman's Reminiscences of Six Years in Camp with the Texas Rangers, *1928*

We girls rode side saddles in those days but, later on, I was the first woman to ride astride in our part of the state, and you may be sure it caused a stampede among the cowboys and the cattle. One "old-timer" near by observed me on that memorable first occasion, and rising in his saddle, with his long white whiskers flying in the breeze, his arms outstretched, exclaimed, "My God! I knew she'd do it! Here she comes wearin' the britches!" My own husband viewed me with surprise, but had no time to comment as he had to get busy and help round up the distracted cattle. Well, I galloped back home as fast as I could and that ended the initial display of my new riding breeches and boots which my mother had just sent me as a gift.

> *Mary Bunton, in* A Bride on the Old Chisholm Trail *in 1886*

You do get in some awful wrecks, though. One time a horse bucked me off that I'd ridden dozens and dozens and dozens of times before. I don't know how come he bucked me off. The whistle had already blew, but he was one the longer you rode him, the harder he bucked. He bucked me right over his head and I lit just sitting up on the ground. He was kicking, of course, and he hit me right between the eyes with his foot. If my head hadn't been coming back, why I guess it would have took my head off. But he just hit me hard enough to black my eyes. But oh! I had the blackest eyes.

> *Barbara Inez "Tad" Lucas, champion rodeo rider from the 1920s until she retired in 1958*

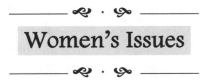

Women's Issues

Mrs. M———, the Texas Diana, has killed with the rifle eighty deer and one buffalo. Her canting husband wanting industry and capacity, she was compelled thus to support him and her children. She now lives alone with her children, in the prairie near Chocolate Bayou...She is a strong active woman not yet thirty. When she hunts, not being able to lift a whole deer, she divides the animal with a "tomahawk" into quarters, tying two of them together, and then suspending them on each side of her horse.

> *Mary Austin Holley,* Texas, *1836*

Who wants a wife with fifteen thousand dollars and the biggest leg in Mexico? Come, my beauties, don't all speak at once. Who is the lucky man?

> *Sarah "The Great Western" Bowman, looking for a husband among a company of dragoons, 1848*

IMPORTANCE OF A SINGLE VOTE

Each of our friends, before thinking of emigrating to Texas, or any other State, ought to take the vote of his wife. The importance of her vote will be felt hereafter; for remember, that a great deal depends on the wife to insure success in a new country. It is she that creates the new home in a strange country; therefore, before you remove, be sure to secure her vote. Remember that the destinies of nations have depended on a single vote. If the question was asked, What caused the Mexican War? the answer would be, The annexation of Texas. What gave us California, Utah and New Mexico? What placed Zachary Taylor in the Presidential Chair? And last, although not least, What may save our glorious Union? The same answer to each of these inquiries must be given:—The annexation of Texas. But how was this annexation of Texas consummated? By ONE VOTE in the United States Senate; and that was cast by Mr. Hannegan of Indiana! How was Mr. Hannegan elected a Senator? By the vote of Mr. Madison Marsh, of Stanton county, Indiana! What majority had Mr. Marsh, by which he was sent so fortunately to the Legislature? ONE VOTE—which was the whole majority he received. As such is the case, and such important results have sprung from that ONE vote, be sure you obtain THAT VOTE from YOUR WIFE; for perhaps, so far as you are concerned, equal results will spring therefrom.

> *Jacob de Cordova,* Texas: Her Resources and Her Public Men, *1858*

A couple of the fort's leading ladies indulged in a fist fight this morning, the result of differences among the children.

> *From the diary that schoolteacher Samuel P. Newcomb kept at Fort Davis, 1865*

There were three saloons, a dance hall, a Chinese laundry, and a restaurant... The restaurant was run by Tom O'Laughlin and wife, Helen, who was the only virtuous woman in town.

> *Mobeetie postmaster George Montgomery, 1879*

My wife has not yet informed me what she will allow me to allow her to become.

> *William Cowper Brann,* The Iconoclast

In bowing her acknowledgements, Miss Bloodgood had the misfortune to spill herself out of her corsage, upon which a fair debutante from Temple, with the naïveté of a little child, observed *sotto voce*, that "a bust of that kind should be carried in a bucket."

> *William Cowper Brann,* The Iconoclast

Mrs. Top, you're the greatest shot I've ever seen.

> *Annie Oakley to professional markswoman Elizabeth "Plinky" Toepperwein*

...any male person in the City of Houston who shall stare at, or make what is commonly called "goo-goo eyes" at, or in any other manner look at or make remarks to or concerning, or cough or whistle at, or do any other act to attract the attention of any woman or female person...

> *Houston ordinance making flirting a misdemeanor, 1905*

Elizabeth "Plinky" Toepperwein, whose marksmanship rivaled that of the better-known Annie Oakley, is seen here dressed for an exhibition.

Texas State Library and Archives Commission

We can conceive of no spectacle more pitiable than a woman grown callous to the sufferings of others, and the evidence of such callousness finds its strongest exhibition in driving recklessly through crowded streets and running down helpless pedestrians, without even halting at the cry of distress in the wake of such mad driving.

> Houston Post, *1905*

I wish to state that I will stop going out and doing any more hard work after my 72nd birthday. Mrs. Mary Bassett.

> *Personal ad,* Dalhart Texan, *1918*

Me and God have an understanding.

> *Lillie Drennan of Hempstead—the "dry land Tugboat Annie"—legendary truck driver and owner of the Drennan Truck Line from 1929 to 1952, dismissing critics of her profanity-laced speech*

I sure hated to pop a cap on a woman.

> *Ranger Captain Frank Hamer, after the ambush of Bonnie and Clyde, 1934*

What a fat man says when he leans over to tie his shoelace in a telephone booth.

> *Definition of "oomph," by Denison native Ann Sheridan, the "Oomph Girl," 1935*

It would never have crossed my mind to command an army of women. I never did learn to salute properly or master the 30-inch stride.

> *Oveta Culp Hobby, first commander of the Women's Army Corps, organized in 1942*

Not that I never quarrel with McMurtry. He sometimes harbors a touch too much romanticism, especially in his early work. His women strike me as a bit much, too heroic and long-suffering and strong. Too *good*. He sees 'em tough, but seldom does he see 'em mean. And Texas probably has as many mean, bitchy, neurotic women as any place on earth, with the possible exception of Manhattan; there, of course, they've gathered from all points of the compass, while our own crop is largely home-grown. McMurtry recognizes their ability to fight back, to survive in tough country, and knows that Texas women may often be stronger than their men. But I think he misses the extent to which large numbers purely enjoy wrecking and plundering and flashing their stingers.

> *Larry L. King, "Leavin' McMurtry,"* Warning: Writer at Work, *1985*

The women's rights movement is the most vicious, conniving, deceiving movement this country has ever seen next to communism.

> *State Representative Larry Vick, 1974*

There's a pat description of "what every Texas woman wants" that varies a bit from city to city, but the formula that Dallas females have been labeled with goes something like this: "Be a Pi Phi at Texas or SMU, marry a man who'll buy you a house in Highland Park, hold the wedding at Highland Park Methodist (flowers by Kendall Bailey), join the Junior League, send the kids to St. Mark's and Hockaday in the winter and Camps Longhorn and Waldemar in the summer, plus cotillion lessons at the Dallas Country Club, have an unlimited charge account at Neiman's as a birthright but buy almost all your clothes at Highland Park Village from Harold's or the Polo Shop, get your hair done at Paul Neinast's or Lou's and drive a Jeep Wagoneer for carpooling and a

Mercedes for fun." There is a kicker equivalent of this scenario that starts, "Every Texas girl's dream is a double-wide in a Lubbock trailer park..."

> *Molly Ivins, "Texas Women: True Grit and All the Rest,"* Molly Ivins Can't Say That, Can She?, *1991*

Weather is like rape—long as it's inevitable, you might as well lie back and enjoy it.

> *Clayton Williams, soon to be former candidate for governor, 1990*

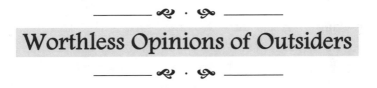

Worthless Opinions of Outsiders

[Texans are] a people whose existence as an independent nation is owing, first, to their own base treason, and secondly, to a political juggle of Andrew Jackson. [Texas is] filled with habitual liars, drunkards, blasphemers, and slanderers; sanguinary gamesters and cold-blooded assassins; with idleness and sluggish indolence (two vices for which the Texans are already proverbial); with pride, engendered by ignorance and supported by fraud.

> *Nicholas Maillard,* The History of the Republic of Texas, *1842*

Some one said that we ought to continue the war and whip them until they consented to take back all Texas.

> *An American soldier writes home about a comrade's proposed terms to end the Mexican War, 1847*

If I owned Texas and all Hell, I would rent out Texas and live in Hell.

> *General Philip Sheridan, 1866*

Several Northern papers are entertaining their readers with stories about Quanah Parker in which the imagination of the writers plays an important part. Among the things we never knew before, they tell us how the Comanche founded the city named after him, and how its inhabitants are prospering by the chief's lavish expenditure of money, he being a multimillionaire. Ring off!

> Quanah Tribune-Chief, *1897*

After living in Texas for ten years I paid a visit to my people beyond the beautiful Ohio. The old gentlemen sized me up critically, evidently expecting to see me wearing war paint and a brace of Bowie knives. "So, young man, You're living in Texas?" "Yes, Paw." "Fell kinder to 'hum 'mong them centerpedes, cowboys 'n other varments, I s'pose?" "Y-y-yes, Paw." "Well, Billy, you allers was a mighty bad boy. I kinder cackalated as how you'd go t'hell some day; but, praise God, I never thought y' was bound for Texas!"

> *William Cowper Brann,* The Iconoclast

The *St. Louis Mirror*, the brightest weekly in the world, recently had a remarkably interesting article on Texas politics; but somehow it suggested to my mind that German metaphysician who, having never seen a lion or read a description of one, undertook to evolve a correct idea of the king of beasts from his own inner consciousness.

> *William Cowper Brann,* The Iconoclast

The Americans are rich in nicknames. Every state has, or has had, its sobriquet. The people of . . . Texas are nicknamed beef-heads.

> *E. Cobham Brewer,* The Dictionary of Phrase and Fable, *1894*

The English get homesick because they cannot get gooseberries and "arf-and-arf" and Lea & Perrin's sauce, growing on every mesquite in Texas. They forget to give any credit to the watermelons, the figs, and other good things that they get in Texas, and that they could not raise, even in a hothouse, in England.

> *Alexander Sweet and J. Armoy Knox,* On a Mexican Mustang Through Texas, *1905*

I always wondered what the inside of a jukebox looked like.

> *Frank Lloyd Wright, on the lurid green decor of the recently opened Shamrock Hotel in Houston, 1949*

They like to hunt for Commies
And pinks of every hue.
But if they can't find Commies,
Plain liberals will do.

> *Skit on Texas and the ultra-conservative Minute Women, staged at the Women's National Press Club, Washington, 1954*

Few documents since the Emancipation Proclamation have stirred as much commotion in Texas as Edna Ferber's novel "Giant," whose protagonists are a pair of Texas millionaires. Ever since the work was published, in 1952, Texans have been denouncing it like sin. The book, they think, slanders not only their millionaires but their state. For an outsider to find a fault in either is, according to the Texas code of conduct, bad form; to knock both is practically an extraditable offense. So it is that, even today, a sojourner in Texas can expect to hear philippics on the evils of ednaferberism.

> *John Bainbridge,* The Super-Americans, *1961*

Houston is spreading like a spilled bucket of water. If something isn't done about it quickly, it will be horrible, horrible.

> *Pierre Voisin,* Houston Post, *1962*

There is a growing feeling that perhaps Texas is really another country, a place where the skies, the disasters, the diamonds, the politicians, the women, the fortunes, the football players and the murders are all bigger than anywhere else.

> *Pete Hamill,* Boston Globe, *after sniper Charles Whitman killed fourteen people on the campus of UT in Austin, 1966*

Houston is six suburbs in search of a center.

> *Nigel Goslin,* Saturday Review, *1967*

In effect, Texas opened the vaults of the U.S. Mint, handed the keys to a bunch of crooks and reckless cowboys, and said, "Come in, y'all."

> *Senator Frank Lautenberg of New Jersey, on the origins of the great Savings & Loan debacle, 1990*

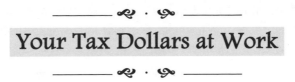

Your Tax Dollars at Work

Republic of Texas:

To all who shall see this present, greeting. Whereas I, Clerk of this County, having this morning unthoughtedly tied my office key as a clapper in my cow's bell; and whereas the said cow has gone astray to parts unknown, bearing with her the said key; and therefore the said key is *non inventus est*—that is, can't be had; And whereas one Abner Barnes has made application to me for marriage license, and the said Abner persists that he cannot wait until the cow comes back with the key, but is compelled, by the violence of his feelings and the arrangements already made, to get married: Therefore these presents are to command any person legally authorized to celebrate the rites of matrimony to join the said Abner Barnes to Rebecca Downs; and for so doing this shall be your sufficient authority.

Given under my hand and private seal, on the doorstep of my office—the seal being locked up, and my cow having gone away with the key—this fourth day of October, A.D. 1838.

Henry Osborne, Clerk.
An improvised marriage license, 1838

Mails.—It is no wonder that these conveyances fail to fulfill the objects designed, since, as we believe, many of the Postmasters are too negligent of their duty to answer in any reasonable degree the purposes of their appointment. We have several times seen, at the opening of the bags here, packages directed to other places in the interior, which had been sent direct opposite their proper route. No longer ago than last Sunday, we saw a package of letters for Henderson, in Rusk County, and two papers for places below this, in this county, going from instead of towards their destination. We do not know how Postmasters regard their oath of office, who are too indolent to look at the table of directions sent to them but dispatch papers and letters any direction, without regard to their duty and the purposes for which they are appointed and paid.

Clarksville Northern Standard, *1844*

No. 6127 Second Class, "B."

PUBLIC DEBT
OF THE
LATE REPUBLIC OF TEXAS

This is to Certify, That David Crockett dec'd per heirs has, under the provisions of An Act of the Legislature of the State of Texas, entitled An Act to extend the provisions of "An Act to provide for ascertaining the Debt of the late Republic of Texas," approved February 7, 1853, filed with the Auditor and Comptroller, A claim for Services at the Alamo in 1836 amounting to Twenty-four Dollars, which is sufficiently authenticated to authorize the auditing of the same under the laws of the late Republic of Texas, Paid in par funds, as having been at that rate so available to the Government.

In Testimony Whereof, We have
hereunto set our hands and affixed
our seals of office at Austin, this 2nd day
of December A.D. 1854

James B. Shaw John M. Swisher
Comptroller Auditor

Eighteen years after her husband's death at the Alamo, Elizabeth Crockett, widow of Davy Crockett, receives a settlement from the State of Texas, which is finally clearing the debts of the old Republic

The undersigned would respectfully represent that in drafting the plan for the Governor's House and necessary outbuildings, the Draftsman consulting the convenience of the outbuildings to the Main Building, placed the *Privy* right opposite the front door of my dwellinghouse, across the street, not thinking of the relative situation it would bear to my home...I never saw the plan and knowing nothing of the position the outbuilding bear to my home, I went to Tennessee, where I was absent some months, & during my absence, the contractor put up the main building & the Privy, which is according to the plan above laid down, right opposite the front door of my house. On returning home I complained to the Building Committee, who said they had not thought of the position the Privy would bear to my house & would be perfectly willing for it to be placed anywhere else, but that all the appropriations made by the last Legislature for the erection of the Governor's House was exhausted, and there were no funds to pay for removing it.

The Privy was removed and rebuilt in another place, by the contractor, I becoming responsible to him for the cost of removing & rebuilding it, which he estimated at one hundred and twentyfive dollars. ($125.00) Had the buildings been those erected by a private individual, throwing the Privy directly in front of my dwellinghouse, there could be no doubt of the duty of that individual to remove it at his own cost and expense. The State should be as just to its citizens, as are individuals with each other, and the undersigned thinks it but just, right, & proper, that a sufficient appropriation be made by the Legislature to pay the necessary expense of removing and rebuilding the Privy, and thereby saving him harmless.

I would refer to the Governor, Comptroller, and Treasurer, to say if the above is not a plain statement of facts.

Joseph Harrell of Austin to the State Legislature, 1856

Condition of the streets of Waco is simply outrageous. The public health is quite in as much danger as the public morals, at least it seems so to a man up in a tree where he goes to get out of the mud. The stench of Austin Street arising from an accumulation of mud and other filth is, under the warm rays of spring sun, fast becoming a nuisance. The attention of the City Fathers is invited to that odorous locality.

Waco Daily Examiner, *1874*

Visited jail and find it lacking in necessary furnishings for comfort of prisoners. The floors are iron and in cold weather not comfortable, for they have no mattresses or anything to shield them from contracting rheumatism and other diseases from sleeping upon a cold iron floor. We therefore recommend the court to supply mattresses for the prisoners.

We think the officials are justly entitled to severe censure for their negligence of allowing prisoners to escape. The jail has been strongly built at great expense to tax payers. We think with due care, on part of those in charge, escape would be impossible. We have ignored finding a bill against them because we believe that escape has been due to want of experience on part of officers, than through criminal intent.

> *Report of the Grand Jury, Mobeetie, 1881 (the signatures including that of Charles Goodnight)*

The dampness of the walls, the exhalations from vapory and various cellars, the leaky roof, and other notable faults, make it unfit for human beings to dwell in.

> Austin Daily Statesman, *on the dilapidated state of the Governor's Mansion, 1883*

Walk your horse over this bridge, or you will be fined.
Schnelles reiten über diese Brücke ist verboten.

Anda despacio con su caballo, ó teme la ley.
Sign at the Commerce Street bridge, San Antonio, 1890s

A STRANGE STORY

In the Northern part of Austin there once dwelt an honest family by the name of Smothers. The family consisted of John Smothers, his wife, himself, their little daughter, five years of age and her parents, making six people toward the population of the city when counted for a special write-up, but only three by actual count.

One night after supper the little girl was seized with a severe colic, and John Smothers hurried downtown to get some medicine.

He never came back.

The little girl recovered and in time grew up to womanhood.

The mother grieved very much over her husband's disappearance, and it was nearly three months before she married again, and moved to San Antonio.

The little girl also married in time, and after a few years had rolled around, she also had a little girl five years of age.

She still lived in the same house where they dwelt when her father had left and never returned.

One night by a remarkable coincidence her little girl was taken with cramp colic on the anniversary of the disappearance of John Smothers, who would now have been her grandfather if he had been alive and had a steady job.

"I will go downtown and get some medicine for her," said John Smith (for it was none other than he whom she had married).

"No, no, dear John," cried his wife. "You, too, might disappear forever and then forget to come back."

So John Smith did not go, and together they sat by the bedside of little Pansy (for that was Pansy's name).

After a little Pansy seemed to grow worse, and John Smith again attempted to go for medicine, but his wife would not let him.

Suddenly the door opened, and an old man, stooped and bent, with long white hair, entered the room.

"Hello, here is grandpa," said Pansy. She had recognized him before any of the others.

The old man drew a bottle of medicine from his pocket and gave Pansy a spoonful.

She got well immediately.

"I was a little late," said John Smothers, "as I waited for a street car."

> *William Sydney Porter, evidently not impressed by the punctuality of Austin's public transportation,* Rolling Stone, *1894*

We're governed entirely too much—Officialism is becoming a veritable Old Man of the Sea on the neck of Labor's Sinbad. About every fifth man you meet is a public servant of some sort, and you cannot get married or buried, purchase a drink or own a dog except with a by-your-leave to the all-pervading law of the land. In some states suicide itself is an infraction of the criminal code, and if the police don't cut you down in time to put you in jail the preachers will send you to hell. Every criminal law this state and county and city needs can be printed in a book no larger than the *Iconoclast*, and that so plain that he who runs may read and reading understand. And when so printed and so understood, without the possibility of misconstruction, they could be enforced at one-fifth the cost of the present judicial failure. We have so many laws and so much legal machinery that when you throw a man into the judicial hopper not even an astrologer can tell whether he'll come out a horse-thief or only a homicide—or whether the people will weary of waiting on the circumlocution office and take a change of venue to Judge Lynch.

> *William Cowper Brann, "Slave or Citizen: the Status of the American Citizen," 1895*

Any person who shall run a horse or mule, or is guilty of fast driving, or speeding a bicycle or automobile, in a manner calculated to endanger persons or property on any of the public streets or alleys of the city of Alpine, shall be fined not less than five or more than one hundred dollars.

Any person who shall engage in any sport or exercise in any public street or highway in this city calculated to scare horses, injure pedestrians or embarrass or retard passage of vehicles, shall be deemed guilty of a misdemeanor.

> *From Ordinance Number 11, Alpine City Commission, 1918*

From each owner or keeper of every kinescope, cinematograph, or similar machine or instrument used for profit which shows the life-like motions of persons or animals, an annual occupation tax of $12.50 shall be collected.

Be it ordained if any person shall within the limits of the City of Groveton throw or cast any stone or other missile upon, against or at any other person, or at any property not belonging to him he shall be guilty of a misdemeanor and upon conviction shall be fined in any amount not exceeding one hundred dollars.

The City Scavenger, twice each month, shall call in person upon each owner or controller of any premises where a privy vault or sink is operated and used and shall collect from the owner thereof, or from the person in control thereof, an assessment at each call, and shall then and there clean out and lime each such privy, vault or sink, and cart away the refuse or offal taken therefrom and dump the same beyond the limits of the city in such manner and at such place or places as will not interfere with the health, comfort, or convenience of any person.

> *Groveton city ordinances, 1919-1920*

Index by Source